93/7/1

B
2

130,00

GUINNESS

THE ULTIMATE RACERS

Alan Cathcart

GUINNESS PUBLISHING

Editor: Honor Head
Pictures: Alan Cathcart
Design and Layout: AdVantage Studios

© Alan Cathcart, 1990

First published in 1990 in Great Britain by
Guinness Publishing Ltd, 33 London Road, Enfield, Middlesex

All rights reserved. No part of this publication may be reproduced, stored in a retrieval system, or transmitted in any form or by any means, electronic, mechanical, photocopying, recording or otherwise, without prior permission in writing of the publisher.

Typeset in Helvetica Light Condensed
by Ace Filmsetting Ltd, Frome, Somerset
Colour origination by
Bright Arts, Hong Kong
Printed and bound in Italy by
New Interlitho SpA, Milan

'Guinness' is a registered trademark of
Guinness Superlatives Ltd

British Library Cataloguing in Publication Data
Cathcart, Alan
Ultimate racers
1. Racing motorcycles, history
I. Title
629.2'275

ISBN 0-85112-916-1

CONTENTS

ACKNOWLEDGEMENTS

No book about racing motorcycles could hope to tell the full story without photographs of the machines themselves, in action and at rest. I am therefore especially glad to have been able to work alongside the following professionals over the years, whose work appears in these pages: Phil Masters, Kel Edge, Emilio Jimenez, John Owens, Ron Lewis, Bill Petro, Claudio Boet, Javier Herrero and Takahashi Akamatsu. To them go my thanks and appreciation for all their collaboration in telling the individual stories of **The Ultimate Racers**.

FOREWORD

I first met Alan Cathcart when he came to Spain to test a bike that I had designed. He impressed me as someone who was more than just another journalist/test rider, as much for his observations about the behaviour of the bike after riding it, as for the depth of the technical questions he asked me about its design. We have seen each other many times since then, and he has tested many of my motorcycles over the years, so it is an especial privilege for me to contribute this foreword to a book written by a person I consider to be the Number One in his profession.

This book traces the technical development of the racing motorcycle from the 350 Garelli of 1924 to the present day, covering forty different machines which, in their own way, contributed to this evolution. I am honoured that one of them is mine, the 250 Kobas 'Twin-Spar'. I have often been asked how I came to design the first Twin-Spar chassis, which when it appeared was so very different from anything seen before, and marked a decisive step in chassis development. I believe the answer is equally applicable to any of my fellow designers, no matter in what field they choose to operate. You simply take a blank sheet of paper and consider critically all the various stages in the design process, however obvious and established the various solutions may appear to be which have been employed up until that time. From this viewpoint, a whole host of ideas will flow, many of them impractical or simply crazy, which after due analysis you then discard. When one of these ideas resists being discarded, and on closer examination proves to have specific merit, then you have the makings of a good solution to your design question. This book is full of examples where such solutions have been found.

I believe that in recent times the design of racing motorcycles has undergone a substantial change in its overall concept. This is due to the development and popularization of computers, utilised in this instance as an intrinsic design element as much as a convenient means of calculation and analysis. In my opinion, this adoption of new techniques has created an important change in the whole philosophy of racing motorcycle development, which has left at a considerable disadvantage those who have not kept pace with it, resulting in an outwardly inexplicable decline in the fortunes of certain marques which previously had been capable of winning races and titles. Whatever the case, the continual advance in the performance of racing bikes is a direct consequence of previous designs which have made their mark, in one way or another, on the overall evolution of the motorcycle.

Antonio Cobas, Barcelona, May 1990.

GARELLI

350 SPLIT-SIN

World 125cc Champion Eugenio Lazzarini demonstrates the Garelli factory's own 350cc split single vintage racer at a Monza historic meeting.

GLE

350 SPLIT-SINGLE

Now that the two-stroke engine in various forms and capacities dominates Grand Prix motorcycle racing so completely, it's fashionable to think that this is only a relatively recent development, the product of Japanese brains and the genius of MZ's Walter Kaaden. Nothing could be further from the truth, for in the early days of GP racing one of Italy's oldest marques swept all before it with an innovative two-stroke machine, which gave the lie to the notion that two-strokes could only ever be humble runabouts incapable of developing race-winning horsepower. The Italian Garelli split-single 350 proved almost unbeatable in its class in the early 1920s, combining speed with reliability to scoop a host of world records. It also achieved innumerable GP victories in the long-distance events of the time, often beating the contestants in the 500cc class which was generally run concurrently in those days. As a result, the Garelli two-stroke became the first Italian motorcycle to gain international racing success, forerunner of so many glorious names like Guzzi, Gilera, MV Agusta and Ducati which would find GP success in decades to come.

Adalberto Garelli was a Milanese inventor with several motorcycle-related patents to his name. In 1913 he designed a radical two-stroke 350cc engine which he put into production in 1919 in a motorcycle bearing his name. The Garelli's engine appeared to be a parallel twin-cylinder design, but in reality the two 50x89mm cylinders (later modified to 52x82mm) shared a common combustion chamber, with a single central conrod bearing a long gudgeon pin which passed through a slot between the two pistons. Both inlet and exhaust

No rear suspension meant a hard ride.

ports were located in the right-hand cylinder, while the transfer ports were cut in the left-hand one, with mixture fed by a single Zenith carburettor, later replaced by a twin-choke unit. The right-hand piston opened the inlet port to transfer mixture from the carburettor to the crankcase, while at bottom dead centre the left-hand piston opened the transfer ports, its domed top helping to force the mixture towards the combustion chamber, where a spark from the single, centrally-mounted plug, fired by the Bosch magneto located in front of the narrow crankcase, ignited it. The burnt gases went down the right-hand cylinder, to escape through the twin exhaust ports and unequal length pipes (which also differed in diameter). The whole design was a fine example of original thought, which delivered 16bhp at 4000rpm in racing form, enough for a top speed of 115kph in road racing trim or, in the form which enabled Garelli to hold 138 world speed records by 1926, over 135kph for short sprints.

One cylinder, two exhaust pipes.

GARELLI 350 SPLIT-

Fitted with a two-speed hand-change gearbox of Garelli's own design, the 350 engine was mounted in a conventional open-cradle single-loop frame, with a rigid rear end and British Druid front girder forks. Only a single drum brake was fitted originally, at the rear, but as speeds rose in 1923 a second, small-diameter drum was added at the front. Remarkably, gear primary drive was employed, with a chain final drive rather than the belt used on the Garelli prewar prototype. Pre-mix fuel in a 6:1 ratio was employed to lubricate the roller and ball-bearing crankshaft as well as the other engine parts, aided where necessary by an auxiliary oil supply carried in a section of the square fuel tank, and delivered by semi-automatic pump.

In this form, the two-stroke Garelli won its first and most gruelling race, the first edition of the Milano-Napoli single-stage marathon (later to become the Milano-Taranto), held in 1919 and won by Ettore Girardi on his 350 split-single, which defeated all 500cc and 1000cc competitors to score an overall victory in this 840km open-roads event. Garelli repeated the feat in 1921 with Ernesto Gnesa, scoring a 1-2-3 win which they repeated the following season in the French GP at Strasbourg with Gnesa again leading his team-mates across the line in formation. Gnesa had already won the first Italian GP, held at Torino in 1921, on the Garelli, but in 1922 he celebrated the opening of the new Monza Autodromo by winning the first-ever GP

Unequal diameter exhaust pipes.

delle Nazioni (the name by which the Italian GP is still known today), defeating the entire 500cc field into the bargain. During the next three years the Garelli team tasted victory wherever they raced, all over Europe, winning the Spanish, Swiss, Austrian, German and Italian GPs on various occasions, as well as the 'Italian TT', the gruelling Circuito del Lario run in the steep hills above Lake Como, and a

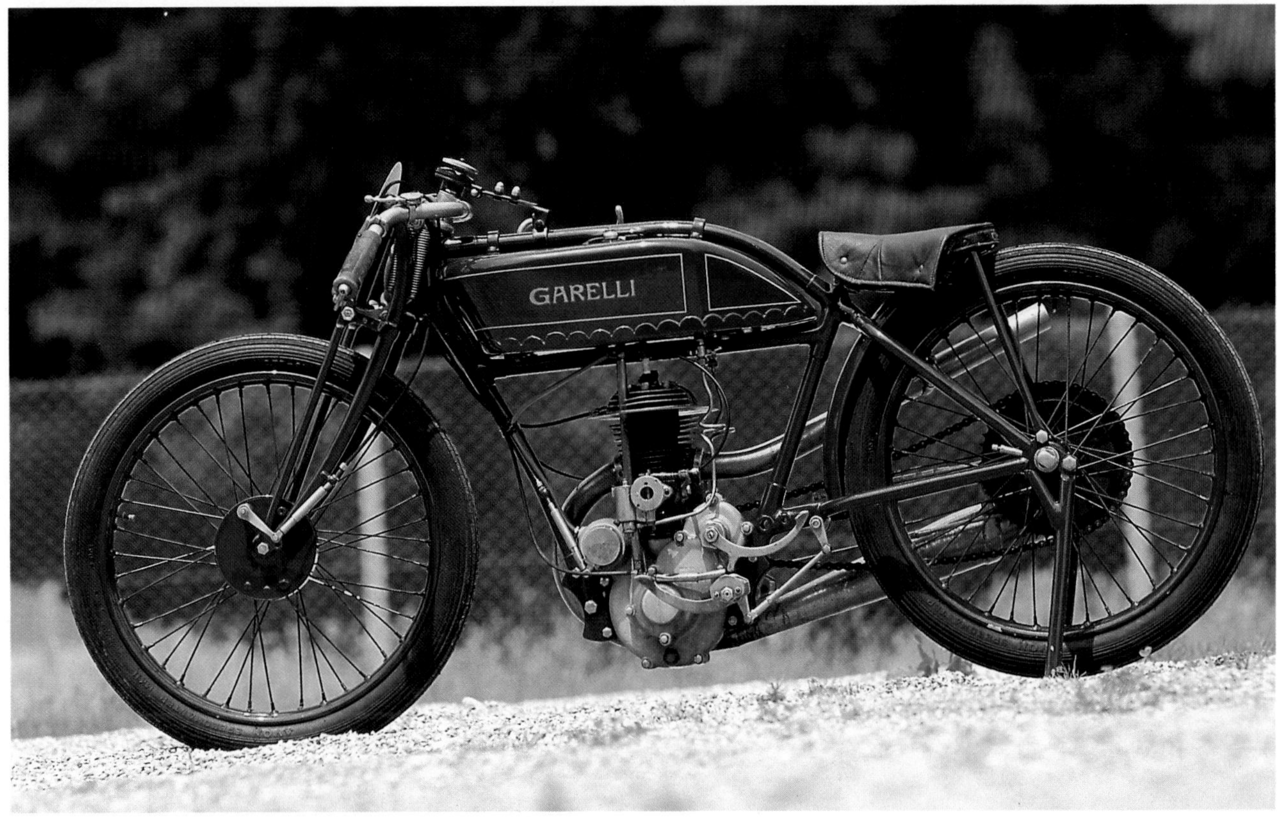

The bicycle origins of the Garelli chassis are clearly evident.

SINGLE

Straddling the Monza startline and six decades, the 350 Garelli faces its 1980s 125 stablemate.

GARELLI 350 SPLIT-

host of Italian national events, including several in the hands of two of Italy's most versatile riders who would later achieve greater fame in Grand Prix car racing, Tazio Nuvolari and Achille Varzi. By 1926, Garelli had little left to prove, so after reaping a new crop of world records at Monza the factory retired from racing for more than half a century before returning with equal, crushing success in the 125cc class in the 1980s.

Strangely, no other manufacturer in Italy attempted to emulate Garelli's feats of two-stroke racing design, and only DKW in Germany and Puch in Austria did so abroad – the former with a similar degree of success before World War II. But Garelli's influence on future two-stroke design was nevertheless important: the use of petroil mixture, gear primary drive and above all experimentation in exhaust pipe shape and length would all prove critical in due course in promoting the two-stroke racing engine to its present position of supremacy.

The front brake provided puny stopping power.

Garelli boss Daniele Agrati (left).

GARELLI 350 SPLIT-SINGLE

Engine: Air-cooled split-single two-stroke

Dimensions: 52x82mm (x2)

Capacity: 348cc

Output: 16bhp at 4000rpm

Carburation: 2x18mm Zenith

Ignition: Marelli magneto

Gearbox: 2-speed with gear primary and hand change

Clutch: Multiplate dry

Chassis: Steel tubular open-cradle single-loop frame

Suspension:
Front: Druid telescopic forks
Rear: None

Brakes:
Front: 120mm single leading-shoe Garelli drum
Rear: Twin 120mm single leading-shoe Garelli drums

Weight: 98kg

Top speed: 70mph

Year of construction: 1924

SINGLE

BIANCHI

350 FRECCIA

The essence of vintage motorcycle racing in action at Misano.

CELESTE

BIANCHI

350 FRECCIA CELESTE

Bianchi were one of the pioneer makes in the history of world motorcycling, evolving from the bicycle factory established in Milan by Edoardo Bianchi in 1885. Today, the marque is still one of the leading Italian brands of pedal cycles with decades of racing success on two wheels to its credit. The first Bianchi to carry an engine appeared in 1890 and thanks to an evolutionary design approach the company became one of the largest Italian motorcycle manufacturers before World War I. Innovative features such as a vertically-posi-

British Druid forks.

Compact engine slots neatly into diamond frame.

tioned engine in 1903, followed by a primitive form of Earles-type front suspension in 1905, founded a reputation for technical ingenuity which would be maintained for several decades.

Bianchi had been involved with road racing both before and after World War I but it was not until 1924 that they produced the machine that was to earn the company fame and success on the tracks. This was the 350cc single-cylinder Freccia Celeste - the so-called 'Sky-Blue Arrow', with its pale blue and white livery that was already a trademark of the Bianchi cycle racing team. This was a highly significant machine in the overall context of racing motorcycle development, for it was certainly the first two-wheeler in Italy and quite possibly anywhere else to boast double overhead-camshaft valve operation with vertical shaft and bevel drive to the cams - a classic form of high-performance engine design which found its ultimate expression in the Manx Norton in the '50s and '60s. At the time that Bianchi designer Mario Baldi produced his 350 single it was a genuine innovation that had hitherto only been experimented with on four-wheeled racing machinery.

Baldi's design employed a single vertical cylinder of relatively short stroke (74x81mm) with both barrel and head made of cast iron, surmounted by a cast aluminium cambox. The rest of the engine was equally innovative for the time, with small-diameter flywheels on the pressed-up crankshaft, automatic oiling and a chain-driven Marelli magneto mounted in front of the crankcase on the right of the engine. Though just a three-speed gearbox with hand change was employed, this had a dry clutch and, while fitted with a chain primary drive, was mounted in a tunnel forming part of the crankcase casting in a semi-unit design which offered superior rigidity while still permitting some degree of adjustment of the primary chain tension. A far-sighted feature was the ability to remove the gearbox internals without disturbing the rest of the engine, simply by unbolting the large end cover on the right side of the casing. Dry sump lubrication was employed, using a small oil tank mounted on the vertical frame member behind the engine, with a supplementary supply in another little receptacle positioned

BIANCHI 350 FRECC

crossways on top of the fuel tank, and a hand pump on the side; in later years, this was converted to primary chain lubrication duties. Running on a 6:1 compression and using a 28mm Dell'Orto carburettor, the 350 Bianchi delivered 22bhp at 5000rpm, a respectable figure for the era which allowed it to exceed 140kph and, allied to a dry weight of 125kg, delivered more than respectable acceleration, especially in later, twin-port mode.

In fact, the 350 Bianchi rapidly proved itself to be more than a match for much larger machines, frequently defeating 500cc and 1000cc bikes in the long-distance events of the day. One such victory was the very first obtained by the prototype Freccia Celeste in 1924, in the Milano–Taranto marathon in the hands of British expatriate Edward Self, surpassed only by the marque's stunning 1-2-3 sweep of the Italian GP run in 1925 at the Monza Autodromo, when the brilliant, gritty Tazio Nuvolari led home team-mates Maffeis and Self to the first of several Bianchi victories in the Italian classic, in the process defeating all the 500cc machines running in a concurrent event. This feat was all the more remarkable considering that Nuvolari had crashed his P2 Alfa Romeo works GP car at high speed at Monza only two weeks before, sustaining numerous cuts and bruises and the odd fracture. Never one to let a little thing like multiple injuries prevent him from racing as successfully on two wheels as he did on four, Nuvolari turned up for the Italian bike GP with his whole upper body encased in a giant plastercast, so that he had to be physically lifted on and off the bike in order to ride it! For this reason, the Bianchi was fitted with a larger-than-usual fuel tank which enabled him to complete the 300km race – entailing around 2½ hours in the saddle – non-stop after being pushstarted from the rear of the grid. In spite of all this he won, and in so doing defeated the cream of European (and British) 350 and 500cc riders in what was that year the European GP.

The 350 Bianchi went on to win the Italian GP no less than five times in succession, as well as the 'Italian TT', the Circuito del Lario, on a record six different occasions. A design which paved the way for a host of two-wheeled imitators in future years, the Bianchi Freccia Celeste was a most significant step in the long evolutionary path of GP motorcycle design.

Distinctive fuel tank design.

BIANCHI 350 FRECCIA CELESTE

Engine: Dohc air-cooled single-cylinder four-stroke

Dimensions: 74x81mm

Capacity: 348cc

Output: 22bhp at 5000rpm

Carburation: 1x28mm Amac

Ignition: Marelli magneto

Gearbox: 3-speed with chain primary and hand change

Clutch: Multiplate dry

Chassis: Tubular steel single-loop open-cradle

Suspension:
Front: Webb girder forks with single spring and twin friction dampers
Rear: None

Brakes:
Front: 180mm single leading-shoe Bianchi drum
Rear: 170mm single leading-shoe Bianchi drum

Weight: 120kg

Top speed: 90mph

Year of construction: 1927

A CELESTE

BMW

500 KOMPRES

Mind the kerb! Flat-twins present ground clearance problems even on skinny tyres.

SOR

BMW

500 KOMPRESSOR

There are numerous claimants for the honour of being the motorcycle that brought road racing design into the modern era, but for many that title goes to the supercharged twin-cylinder BMW Kompressor that won the 500cc European Championship in 1938 in the hands of Georg Meier, as well as a series of GPs in 1938/9, including the Isle of Man Senior TT – the first time it was won by a foreign rider. In the hands of Meier and team-mates Ludwig 'Wiggerl' Kraus and Briton Jock West, the 'blown' BMW was a potent contender for classic honours in the immediate prewar era, as well as setting a world motorcycle speed record in 1937 on the Frankfurt–Munich autobahn in the hands of Ernst Henne. Henne's mark of 279.50kph, set with a developed, streamlined version of the 500 Kompressor, was to stand for 14 years as a mark of the machine's excellence. And with a vanquished Germany not readmitted to the FIM until 1950, the postwar international ban on supercharging was ignored there immediately after the cessation of hostilities, permitting updated Kompressor models to dominate German national racing with ease. Thereafter, it was redesigned into the illustrious, normally-aspirated Rennsport engine, which dominated sidecar racing at all levels for the next quarter-century.

BMW established the lines and performance of the modern motorcycle with this design.

Plunger rear suspension.

The Kompressor engine was designed in 1934 by Rudolph Schleicher as a 180-degree flat-twin which was already set to become the trademark format of the Bavarian firm's motorcycle production, and was first raced the following year. Displaying a cost-no-object approach, like their Auto-Union and Mercedes-Benz compatriots on four wheels, all the major castings in the BMW engine were in lightweight but expensive electron magnesium, even including the cylinder heads. The built-up all-roller-bearing crankshaft was fitted with elliptical conrods carrying four-ring pistons with three compression rings and one scraper, with a magneto chain-driven off the end of the crank via an intermediate shaft, which in turn also drove the twin overhead camshafts via a horizontal shaft and sets of bevel gears. Each pair of camshafts was geared directly to one another with short rockers actuating the valves and hairpin springs for the two valves per cylinder.

At the rear of the crankcase, a separate electron housing was bolted on, containing the four-speed gearbox and single-plate dry clutch, with the shaft final drive that was already a BMW trademark, too. At the front, the outer crankcase cover was fitted with a Zoller eccentric-vane supercharger spline-driven off the nose of the crankshaft. Outputs of the Kompressor engine varied according to the era

BMW 500 KOMPRES

and fuel used, as well as the purpose. Henne's record-breaker yielded around 90bhp, with 65bhp at the crankshaft at 7000rpm on tap for Meier's road racer, both running on specially-blended fuel. Coupled with an exceptionally low dry weight of only 139kg (recorded at the weigh-in for the 1939 Senior TT), this bike gave a brilliant performance for the day surpassed only by Serafini's 'blown' Gilera Rondine four-cylinder, which pipped the BMWs for the 1939 European title, but was neither so flexible nor handled nearly so well as the German twins.

There were two principal reasons for this: firstly, Schleicher's original design, even in its more highly tuned, developed form, avoided the 'sudden death' delivery of most forced induction engines which is as much a feature of modern turbocharged designs (in which the exhaust gases are used to drive a turbo unit to compress the fresh charge) as it was with earlier supercharged engines like the BMW, where an engine-driven compressor carries out the same task. This was achieved by means of an internal redesign of the Zoller unit, thus effecting both displacement and compression via the long induction tubes leading under each cylinder to the rear-facing inlet ports from the supercharger, fed by a single 27mm Fischer-Amal carburettor. This not only ensured the mixture was adequately cooled, but also made for a smooth and tractable power delivery: the Kompressor BMW would pull from as low as 2500rpm, accompanied by the distinctive whine from the 'blower', with a very flat torque curve. This was especially true when the engine was fitted postwar with the larger 'Henne-kompressor' used on the record bike, which delivered more boost at lower revs and smoothed out the power delivery.

In many ways the BMW's trump card was its advanced chassis design, which in spite of the shaft final drive made it much more controllable than its four-cylinder rivals. BMW were pioneers in fitting both telescopic front forks and sprung rear suspension – initially, before World War II, of a plunger type with adjustable friction dampers, then later a proper swinging fork – accompanied by early use of clip-on handlebars and a twin leading-shoe front brake. Though flimsy and unsophisticated by modern standards, BMW's 28mm hydraulically-damped telescopic front forks made the Kompressor handle and steer infinitely better than its girder-forked rivals, ushering in a new era in motorcycle technology that, if only partially, at least enabled chassis design to start catching up with the remarkable power outputs achieved by prewar supercharged engines running on heady brews of exotic fuel. We are still reaping the benefits today.

BMW 500 KOMPRESSOR

Engine: Dohc air-cooled horizontally-opposed twin-cylinder four-stroke

Dimensions: 66x72mm

Capacity: 493cc

Output: 55bhp at 7000rpm (on petrol)

Carburation: Zoller eccentric-vane supercharger fed by single 27mm Fischer-Amal

Ignition: Bosch magneto

Gearbox: 4-speed with gear primary and shaft final drive

Clutch: Single-plate dry

Weight: 139kg

Top speed: 135mph

Year of construction: 1939

Chassis: Tubular steel duplex cradle

Suspension:
Front: 28mm BMW telescopic forks
Rear: BMW plunger suspension units with separate friction dampers

Brakes:
Front: 200mm twin leading-shoe BMW drum
Rear: 200mm single leading-shoe BMW drum

VELOCETTE KTT MARK

High-set riding position was a distinctive KTT trademark.

VIII

KTT MARK VIII

Though occasional forays were made into the 250 and 500cc classes with variations on the same theme, the old-established British Velocette concern concentrated on the 350cc class during their quarter-century in international road racing. This culminated in successive 350cc titles in the first two years that the world championships were inaugurated in 1949/50, courtesy of Freddie Frith and Bob Foster, with special factory 'double-knocker' versions of the legendary sohc Velocette KTT

Webb girders.

Mark VIII Velo was for many the prettiest British racing bike ever built.

Mark VIII which for many years was the preferred choice of privateers around the world for the 350 racing category.

One of the prettiest racing bikes ever built, the Mark VIII KTT was the last in a long line of Velocette production racers descended from the company's first ohc machine, which made its debut in the 1925 Isle of Man Junior TT. Previously best known for their range of efficient but scarcely performance-orientated two-stroke lightweights, Velocette's entry into the racing arena with a 74x81mm 348cc four-stroke (these dimensions were to be retained for all future KTT variations) caused some surprise, though the subsequent retirement of all three machines entered did not. But Velocette obviously profited from the experience, for the following year they returned to register the first-ever TT victory for an overhead-camshaft machine when Alec Bennett won the 350cc Junior TT at record speed on his works entry. He repeated his victory in 1928, with team-mate Freddie Hicks the winner in '29, to complete a hat-trick of Velocette TT wins. In the meantime, Velocette rider Frank Longman had won the 1927 French 350 GP, to score the firm's first of many victories outside Britain.

This success encouraged the Goodman company who owned Veloce Ltd, makers of the Velocette, to produce the first genuine production racing motorcycle (as opposed to tuned roadster) to be offered for sale to the British public. The Mark I KTT, which appeared in 1929, was in every way a customer version of the company's TT-winning works racers – hence the 'KTT' label: probably in view of the Goodmans' German antecedents all Velocette overhead-camshaft models bore the letter 'K'. During the 1930s, the KTT was gradually updated and refined, scoring literally hundreds of race wins all over the world in the hands of its satisfied customers. Thanks to the capacity for original thought of chief engineer Harold Willis (a man also endowed with an endearing turn of phrase, who gave the world the 'double-knocker' epithet for twin overhead camshafts!), Velocette were in the vanguard of technical development in the prewar era. They were the first to fit the positive-stop foot gearchange soon to be universally adopted,

VELOCETTE KTT M

among the first to use what was then quaintly termed a 'sprung frame' (with rear suspension), and again one of the first to enclose the valve-springs, which greatly added to the clean look of their engines – both before a race and after!

For the 1938 season the Mark VII version of the KTT was introduced, with a new engine featuring a large one-piece alloy casting combining cylinder head and cambox in one, with enclosed hairpin valve-springs and a single overhead camshaft driven by the KTT's traditional method of vertical shaft and bevel gears. Fitted with eccentrically-adjustable rockers and a massively finned cylinder, the 348cc engine yielded 27bhp at 6500rpm running on a 50/50 petrol/benzol mixture, though with improved fuel and a higher compression ratio after the post-World War II 'pool' petrol era had ended, this could be raised to 34bhp at 7000rpm in Mark VIII KTT form. Combined with a four-speed gearbox with chain primary drive – surprisingly, Willis's visionary talents did not encompass a gear primary – the new engine was fitted in a rigid version of the works racers' 'spring frame' designed in accordance with the wishes of Velocette's current works rider – the legendary Irishman, Stanley Woods – with a single top tube and vertical down tube, bifurcating into a twin-loop engine cradle. Only 25 examples or so of this rigid-frame interim model were made before being superseded by the ultimate version of the KTT Velocette, the Mark VIII, which appeared at the end of 1938 and was practically identical to the works machine on which Woods had won the '38 Junior TT – a feat he would repeat in 1939.

In this final form, always fitted with girder front forks (which were to become a postwar anachronism: Velocette were the last major manufacturer to retain them) and Dowty springless oleopneumatic rear suspension units, the Mark VIII KTT dominated 350cc racing in the immediate postwar era, winning a great many races all over Europe, as well as three successive IoM Junior TTs and, in dohc 'double-knocker' form, those two world titles. Had Velocette chosen to update the cycle parts, it seems probable that this enviable record could have been maintained for at least another couple of seasons, but the introduction of the Featherbed Norton chassis in 1950 only underlined the prewar nature of the Velocette frame. Had Harold Willis not tragically died in 1939, it seems unlikely that this situation would have arisen, but as it is the KTT Velocette will be remembered as the ultimate British 350 of the pre-World War II era, which helped to rekindle the racing flame after the war ended and the world struggled to its feet again.

Offset revcounter.

VELOCETTE KTT MARK VIII

Engine: Sohc air-cooled single-cylinder four-stroke

Dimensions: 74x81mm

Capacity: 348cc

Output: 34bhp at 7000rpm

Carburation: 1x1 3/32 inch Amal 10TT

Ignition: BTH magneto

Gearbox: 4-speed with chain primary

Clutch: Multiplate dry

Chassis: Tubular steel cradle

Suspension:
Front: Webb girder forks with single spring and twin friction dampers
Rear: Tubular steel swingarm with twin Dowty Oleopneumatic units

Brakes:
Front: 7 inch twin leading-shoe Velocette drum
Rear: 7 inch single leading-shoe Velocette drum

Weight: 145kg

Top speed: 115mph

Year of construction: 1948

ARK VIII

GILERA

SATURNO 50

Gilera factory museum's Saturno has been well-restored for vintage events.

0 SANREMO

GILERA

SATURNO 500 SANREMO

Few motorcycles have proved such effective all-rounders as the British BSA Gold Star and the Italian Gilera Saturno – both pushrod ohv single-cylinder four-strokes with a curiously parallel lifeline. Both were born in the immediate prewar era, both blossomed in the '40s and '50s in a huge variety of sporting disciplines, as well as carving a niche for themselves as the most desirable of mile-eating roadsters, and both were eventually over-shadowed by supposedly more pure bred designs. Maybe that's also why both are prized collector's items today!

The BSA was almost equally at home off road as on, whereas the Gilera's ability was slightly slanted towards road-racing events – although its versatility could hardly be questioned. Winner of numerous gold medals in the ISDT Six Days events, a fearsome dirt sled in early Italian motocross racing, and victor of dozens of sidecar events on and off the road, the Saturno actually evolved from the pre-World War II 'otto bulloni' (eight stud) VT (overhead valve) roadbike, from which Gilera designer Giuseppe Salmaggi developed a 500cc racer. This won its very first competitive outing in the 1940 Targa Florio in the hands of works rider Massimo Masserini.

The new model, named the Saturno as part of Gilera's 'galaxy' of machines (others were called the Nettuno, Mars and suchlike – but no Venus!), differed from the VL in having a unit-construction gearbox with gear primary drive, and was distinguished by its ultra-clean aesthetics, with polished alloy castings and all-internal oilways. During World War II, various military versions helped to assure the reliability of the big Gilera ohv single, so

Gilera made their own brakes, too.

that when bike racing began again in Italy in 1946, generally around twisty street circuits, the flexible, torquey but dependable Saturno was frequently able to defeat more powerful, but less user-friendly rivals. When Carlo Bandirola won the opening GP of the 1947 season on one of the factory development bikes, the Saturno racer was dubbed the 'Sanremo' after the town in which this victory was earned, to distinguish it from its roadster sister which had recently been launched. In this form, fitted with blade-type girder forks and a spring frame which utilized Gilera's own highly original form of rear suspension (twin horizontal springs enclosed in the rear frame tubes, controlled by friction dampers), the Sanremo scored countless victories both in Italy and abroad during the next five years. While their new unsupercharged 500cc four-cylinder air-cooled works machine was under development, Gilera ran a completely separate race department in the Arcore factory which provided works riders with single-cylinder Saturno steeds for Italian national events, as well as the occasional overseas race. One such provided the

Clean lines epitomise Gilera's design philosophy.

GILERA SATURNO

Saturno's most famous victory, the 1950 Spanish GP at Montjuich Park, won by Nello Pagani on his own Sanremo.

In due course Gilera bowed to modern developments and converted the Saturno to more conventional telescopic front forks and a swinging-arm rear end with separate suspension units, in which form the bike was known as the 'Piuma', or feather. Like the contemporary 'Featherbed' Norton, this nickname was for the improved nature of its ride rather than any weight reduction, since in this final (1952) form, the Sanremo weighed 128kg dry, versus 120kg in its previous form. But with the output from the 84x90mm long-stroke engine, fitted with a 35mm Dell'Orto carburettor, and forward-mounted Bosch magneto gear-driven off the roller-bearing crankshaft, now increased to 38bhp at 6000rpm in final Piuma form, the Gilera was still able to give a good account of itself on tortuous tracks against more modern, less versatile bikes. This was thanks in no small measure to the massive reserves of torque from the lusty engine and the great flexibility provided by the straight pipe, in contrast to the fussier performance of more powerful 'cammy' designs fitted with megaphone exhausts.

Though by comparison with the more refined chassis of its British rivals the Gilera looked back to the '30s rather than ahead to the '60s, its engine design was not only much cleaner but also more modern than the British singles, with their exposed, oil-leaking valve-springs and chain primary drives. Only the Sanremo's pushrod valve-gear was humble by comparison with the Manx Norton's dohc design, but even here the Italian factory remedied this by introducing the ultimate version of the Saturno engine, the twin-cam Bialbero with gear-driven dohc cylinder head. Sadly, the double-knocker Saturno never achieved its full potential. A series of outings in the hands of various riders during 1953 culminated in a solitary victory for Frenchman Georges Monneret in a Bordeaux street race before the increasing nimbleness of the four-cylinder works bikes (after Geoff Duke's arrival in the factory team dramatically improved their handling) put paid to the Bialbero's only real advantage over the fours – its better performance on tight tracks. This was a pity, for a gear-drive conversion to the pushrod Sanremo production racer would have enabled its owners to remain competitive against the heavier but more powerful British singles for some years to come. Instead, the Saturno remained an honourable second best at international level – but still a great all-rounder.

GILERA SATURNO 500 SANREMO

Engine: Air-cooled pushrod ohv single-cylinder four-stroke

Dimensions: 84x90mm

Capacity: 499cc

Output: 38bhp at 6000rpm

Carburation: 1x35mm Dell'Orto

Ignition: Bosch magneto

Gearbox: 4-speed with gear primary

Clutch: Multiple oilbath

Chassis: Steel tubular open-cradle with duplex top and single down tubes

Suspension:
Front: 35mm Gilera telescopic forks
Rear: Steel tubular swingarm with twin Koni units

Brakes:
Front: 220mm single leading-shoe Gilera drum
Rear: 185mm single leading-shoe Gilera drum

Weight: 128kg

Top speed: 120mph

Year of construction: 1953

MOTO GUZZI

500 BICILIND

A true original – the wide-angle 120-degree Guzzi in 1951 guise. This particular bike was rediscovered in Brazil, where it had ended its racing days.

RICA

500 BICILINDRICA

Few, if any, Grand Prix motorcycles have ever approached the longevity record of Moto Guzzi's 120-degree V-twin racer, which also proved almost instantly successful. It won the 1934 Spanish GP in the hands of Stanley Woods, yet no less than 18 years later took victory in the Swiss GP in its final season at world championship level, ridden

Leading-link front suspension.

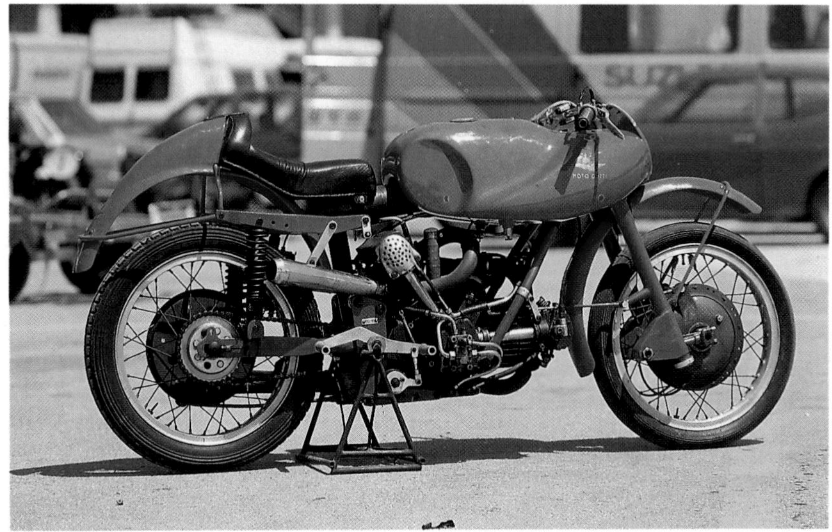

'Anatomical' fuel tank was a typical '50s feature.

by Fergus Anderson. The idea of a works racer that, albeit with updated chassis designs over the years, remained substantially unchanged in terms of its engine format over a two-decade period, is almost unthinkable today. Times have changed, and so has the pace of technical evolution.

Part of the reason for the Guzzi's Methuselah-type lifespan was its original avant-garde design: when it first appeared in 1934, the Guzzi Bicilindrica was the first racing motorcycle to feature swinging-arm rear suspension, in due course to become a standard feature of all two-wheelers. Yet its creation came about as a response to the conservative, and thus unsuccessful nature of Guzzi's pushrod four-cylinder design of the early '30s, which though supercharged, was too heavy and underpowered to be competitive. Designer Carlo Guzzi therefore hit on the idea of fitting an extra cylinder to the successful 250cc Albatros horizontal-single machine to scale it up into a full 500. The idea worked, and the wide-angle air-cooled V-twin was born.

In order to cool the rear cylinder adequately, the Guzzi's included cylinder angle was an unusual 120 degrees – never done before or since – but like the 90-degree V-twin Ducati 40 years later, employing differential cylinder finning to maximize the cooling effect. The 120-degree angle would have resulted in vibration had Guzzi not fitted offset crankpins to ensure evenly-spaced firing intervals, a concept favoured by the Japanese for their V-twin roadsters half a century later. Drive to the single overhead camshaft per cylinder was by vertical shaft and bevel gears off the right side of the crankshaft from an external housing, to which the two-way oil pump was also attached for the dry-sump oil system, with the oil tank perched above the fuel reservoir in what was by now the traditional Guzzi manner. The Bosch magneto was mounted

One of the few.

between the cylinders, and rather surprisingly in view of the wide included angle, the wheelbase of the rigid frame, fitted with Brampton girder forks, was lengthened by only 25mm, compared to the single-cylinder 250, to just 1390mm. Though remarkably compact for a wide-angle V-twin 500, this meant that the rear one of the two 28.5mm Dell'Orto carbs was positioned some way behind the rider's left leg, level with the rear wheel rim. Design of the individual cylinders was similar to the 250, with typically 'square' Guzzi dimensions of 68x68mm – another innovative move in an era of longstroke designs. Fitted with a four-speed, foot-change gearbox and weighing 151kg dry, the new 500 Guzzi produced 44bhp at 7000rpm – compared to the 250 Albatros's 22bhp at 7500rpm and a dry weight of 132kg.

The Guzzi Bicilindrica was a winner from the start, Woods' Spanish GP victory being followed by four wins in succession in the gruelling Milano-Napoli marathon from 1934-7. During the same period, the Bicilindrica tasted success all over Europe, winning the Italian GP at Monza three times in a row from 1934-6, thanks to a top speed of over 180kph on the banked circuit. But the bike's most famous victory came in 1935, when the 500 Moto Guzzi in the hands of Stanley Woods became the first non-British machine to win a race in the Isle of Man since Godfrey's Indian in 1911; Woods won the Senior TT by a mere four seconds from Guthrie's works Norton single. By this time, the V-twin engine had been fitted in a revised chassis with Guzzi's own triangulated swinging-fork rear suspension, controlled by horizontal springs and friction dampers, whose damping rate could be varied during the course of a race as the fuel load lightened by a cable-operated preload adjuster mounted on the underside of the fuel tank – yet another innovative Guzzi feature which only reappeared on modern

120-degree engine employs bevel drive to the sohc valve gear, like later Ducati 90-degree V-twins.

CILINDRICA

Well-restored example of original 1935 Bicilindrica design.

MOTO GUZZI 500 B

GP bikes in the mid-1980s.

Though by 1938 the Guzzi's output had been raised to 47bhp at 7500rpm, the advent of the supercharged 'multis' like the rival Gilera and BMW made it uncompetitive, in spite of its light weight and nimble handling. But after World War II, with the subsequent ban on supercharging, the Guzzi Bicilindrica enjoyed a new lease of life while Gilera, for example, had to come up with a new design to replace their 'blown' four. Guzzi dominated the postwar Italian championship up until 1950 with a revised version of the prewar bike, which featured a new chassis which would set the trend for future Guzzi racers. It had a large-diameter central tubular backbone which also doubled as the oil tank: years later, this would be known as an 'Egli frame' after the Swiss special builder, when really it was a Guzzi design! Telescopic forks were now fitted, later replaced by a leading-link front end that again would be copied on the factory's title-winning 1950s bikes, while careful engine development brought the power output up to 45bhp again (now at 8000rpm) in spite of the compression being dropped to take into account the poor quality of the fuel available immediately after the war.

In this final form the Guzzi Bicilindrica nearly won another Senior TT in 1949, when Bob Foster led until the penultimate lap when the 'bacon-slicer' outside flywheel sheared off. In 1951, power was increased to 52bhp at 8000rpm, and the top speed through the Monza speed trap to 210kph – some going for an 18-year-old design! But it was the V-twin's traditional attributes of a smooth power delivery and easy handling that enabled Fergus Anderson to clinch the model's final GP victory in the pouring rain on a twisty circuit at Bern, Switzerland. It was the swansong of a great motorcycle.

Swing arm is flimsy by today's standards.

MOTO GUZZI 500 BICILINDRICA

Engine: Sohc air-cooled 120-degree V-twin four-stroke

Dimensions: 68x68mm

Capacity: 494cc

Output: 52bhp at 8000rpm

Carburation: 2x35mm Dell'Orto

Ignition: Scintilla magneto

Gearbox: 4-speed with gear primary

Clutch: Multiplate dry

Chassis: Steel tubular spine frame with sheet steel cradle and twin downtubes

Suspension:
Front: Moto Guzzi leading-link telescopic forks
Rear: Steel tubular swingarm with twin Koni dampers

Brakes:
Front: 220mm twin leading-shoe Moto Guzzi drum
Rear: 210mm single leading-shoe Moto Guzzi drum

Weight: 145kg

Top speed: 120mph

Year of construction: 1951

CILINDRICA

NORTON MANX 500

The author aboard the 1962 ex-Malcolm Uphill Manx now owned by Ian Telfer – one of the last of an illustrious line of Norton racers.

NORTON

MANX 500

The Manx Norton has few rivals as the archetypal British single-cylinder racer, and only the later TZ Yamaha can match its widespread appeal and formidable record of success over so extended a period. Indeed, the Manx's popularity and racing success imbued the Norton marque with an aura of quality that extended right down to their humblest roadster in a way few other marques have ever managed – which, after all, is one of the principal commercial justifications for going racing in the first place! At one time in the 1950s, due to the efforts of the factory race team which won three

The Telfer Norton, twice winner of the Ray Petty Trophy.

world titles in the hands of Geoff Duke, 1951/2, Norton on two wheels held a similar place in the consciousness of the British public at large as Jaguar held on four wheels through their Le Mans 24-Hour sports car victories. In Norton's case this was achieved, and maintained, by a brave if stubborn defiance of the inevitable, represented by the 'foreign' multi-cylinder designs from Italy and Germany which were increasingly successfully challenging Norton's dominance in GP racing. In other words, the single-cylinder Norton represented a gallant example of the traditional British love of the underdog, so that even after the factory team retired from racing at the end of 1955, Norton's image was safe in the hands of the hundreds of privateers, from all nations and in many different countries, who continued to race with steady success on Manx Nortons up till the early '70s.

These privateers came to appreciate the qualities of the dohc Manx Norton, which on a winter's rebuild at the start of each season combined with periodic maintenance throughout the year, would yield a whole season of road racing in the GPs and at lucrative non-championship international events. The so-called 'Continental Circus', a cosmopolitan group of privateer racers, the majority of whom were equipped with a brace of British singles (the 500 invariably a Manx Norton and the 350 either that or a 7R AJS) sprang up in the postwar era and flourished in the more prosperous '60s. This was when many of its members discovered that the entry dues to fame and fortune aboard a Japanese factory's small-capacity, multi-cylinder projectile were invariably paid by making your name in the 350 and 500cc classes aboard a British single. Even as the production racing fruits of that decade of Japanese racing involvement

Four leading-shoe front brake.

High-rise exhaust is a period modification.

NORTON MANX 500

The ultimate British single-cylinder racing engine.

began to elbow the Norton and its kin from contention in first the 350, then the 500cc categories, the Norton hung on to pack the grids and provide more carefree, if less competitive racing. The labour-intensive maintenance and seizure-prone comportment of the TR Yamaha and H1R Kawasaki made racing more of a chore than a sport in the early '70s.

A non-standard belt-drive primary.

It was the inadequate handling of these early Japanese two-stroke production racers that set them aside from the Manx and its kin, for nothing before or since has handled as well as the Norton's twin-loop, double-cradle 'Featherbed' frame, introduced in 1950 on the works racers and subsequently adopted by all the customer machines built until 1962 when production ceased. So named by works rider Harold Daniell after his first test ride aboard the McCandless-designed chassis, the Featherbed's legendary road-holding was responsible in no small part for the Norton's unparalleled record of racing success. It set new standards in

Former world champion John Surtees en route to second place in the 1986 French Historic GP on his own Manx. Box section swingarm is non-standard.

NORTON MANX 500

steering and stability, especially compared to the previous single-tube 'Garden Gate' Manx chassis, which in postwar form with plunger rear suspension was the first true Manx Norton. Prewar customer racers were dubbed the 'International', the same as the single overhead camshaft roadsters they closely resembled.

The Norton works team were actually equipped with twin-cam cylinder heads as early as 1937 for their long-stroke, 79x100cc engines the initial design of which by Walter Moore dated back to 1927. Brilliant work by Norton's development engineer Joe Craig had resulted in continual improvements to this basic design, so that by the mid-'30s the Norton factory team dominated the 500cc class both on the Isle of Man and in the European GPs. The advent of the supercharged multis dented this dominance for a while just before the outbreak of World War II, but the subsequent ban on supercharging restored Norton to its previous position when racing began again in 1947, which the introduction of the Featherbed frame in 1950 only confirmed.

Joe Craig had varied the bore and stroke dimensions of the works bikes over the years, and in 1954 a long-overdue change in the configuration of the production Manx engines was made, the 500 adopting almost 'square' dimensions of 86x85.8mm, and the 350 76x76.7mm. This did give the model a new lease of life at privateer level, but by then the modern era had well and truly arrived in the form of the four-cylinder Italian Gileras, to which Norton's star rider Geoff Duke had defected after winning the third of his, and Norton's, world titles in the 350cc class in 1952. Duke's joining Gilera, and his subsequent importation of Norton's chassis technology to Italy, yielded him a further three world titles on the Italian bikes, while Joe Craig's increasingly futile loyalty to his beloved singles ensured that Norton never again won a world title. It is debatable whether this was due to Craig's stubbornness, or the refusal of the board of Associated Motor Cycles to which Norton now belonged, to fund a multi-cylinder project. But it's certain that Craig tried to acquire the rights to the French-built four-cylinder Nougier machine, as well as drawing up the outline of a water-cooled Norton four in-house. However, all this was cut short when Norton pulled out of racing on an official basis, and left their customers to carry the company flag on the Manx production racers. This they did to good effect, aided by the efforts of such legendary tuners as Francis Beart, Ray Petty, Steve Lancefield and many more. Thanks to them and the thousands of riders who have raced a Manx Norton at one time or another since then, right up to the present day, the legendary reputation of one of the greatest motorcycles of all time has been amply sustained. The Manx may be gone, but it is not forgotten.

NORTON MANX 500

Engine: Dohc air-cooled single-cylinder four-stroke

Dimensions: 86x85.8mm

Capacity: 498cc

Output: 54bhp at 7200rpm

Carburation: 1x1½ inch Amal GP

Ignition: Lucas magneto

Gearbox: 4-speed with chain primary

Clutch: Multiplate dry

Chassis: Steel tubular duplex cradle

Suspension:
Front: Norton Roadholder telescopic forks
Rear: Steel tubular swingarm with twin Girling units

Brakes:
Front: Dual 7 inch twin leading-shoe Norton drum
Rear: 7 inch single leading-shoe Norton drum

Weight: 140kg

Top speed: 140mph

Year of construction: 1962

GILERA 500 FOUR

World 500cc champion in 1950 and 1952 aboard the works' four-cylinder Gilera, Umberto Masetti is seen here in action on a later model at Misano in 1986.

500 FOUR

The 1950s were a golden age for Grand Prix motorcycle racing, especially in the 500cc class where half-a-dozen manufacturers contested the newly-instituted world championship series on a variety of increasingly sophisticated machines whose design influence is still felt today. This is especially true of the air-cooled, transverse in-line four-cylinder Italian Gileras, with twin overhead camshafts driven up the centre of the engine. Though at the time they first appeared, the Gileras' design seemed incredibly complex and avant-garde, in the course of time it would come to represent the epitome of the UJM – the Universal Japanese Motorcycle for the street. Thus was convention born out of innovation.

Ultimate development of the four-cylinder line, this 1957 model is now housed in the Gilera factory museum.

Gilera made all their own forks and brakes.

Gilera dominated the 500cc GPs until their abrupt departure from the racing scene, in company with Moto Guzzi and Mondial, at the end of the 1957 season. Already winners of the final European title to be run before World War II broke out, with the water-cooled, supercharged Rondine design they had acquired from the Roman CNA design partnership, Milan's family-owned Gilera concern – Italy's oldest manufacturer, born in 1909 – originally ran the same bike in the early postwar era, but shorn of its supercharging. This was only a stop-gap measure, pending the arrival of an all-new, unblown design which made its debut in 1948, and went on to win six world championships during the next nine years in the hands of Umberto Masetti, Libero Liberati and the great Geoff Duke, as well as becoming the first machine to lap the Isle of Man TT course at more than 100mph, in the hands of Bob McIntyre in 1957. Only Duke's brilliance aboard the underpowered but better-handling Manx Norton singles prevented Gilera from making a clean sweep of the world 500cc titles during their years in contention.

The 1950s were therefore Gilera's golden era, too, when Duke, Masetti, Armstrong, McIntyre, Pierre Monneret, McCandless, Bob Brown, Liberati, Nello Pagani and Alfredo Milani – not to mention the

Seven-speed gearbox.

GILERA 500 FOUR

efforts of Albino Milani and, later on, Florian Camathias, aboard Gilera-engined sidecar outfits – took the red-and-white four-cylinder machines from the Arcore factory to a host of victories against keen opposition from MV Agusta, Norton, Guzzi, AJS and BMW. Unlike in later years, when Count Agusta's machines had a relatively unchallenged ride to one world title after another

A four megaphone exhaust.

(always excepting Agostini's first two championship wins in 1966/7 against Hailwood on the Honda), the Gileras had to battle to prove their worth, and the success they enjoyed confirms their position as not only the genesis, but also the cream of the four-cylinder racing crop.

Such comparison with the MVs of the 1950s is all the more valid given that both machines were designed by the same man, Pietro Remor. Originally responsible for the supercharged Rondine, Remor was required by the postwar ban on supercharging to design a completely new Gilera machine, which he based on an abortive 250cc blown four he had drawn up in 1940. But before the new design could prove its worth, Remor defected to the fledgling Agusta team, for whom he designed a carbon copy engine which, initially at least, failed to match the Gilera's performance due to the succession of bad-handling chassis it was installed in.

The Gileras didn't handle much better, but with the arrival of Geoff Duke in the team in 1953 a definite improvement was registered which made the bikes

Longstroke in-line four-cylinder engine is quite compact.

The Gilera at Monza – a short stone's throw from home base.

GILERA 500 FOUR

well-nigh unbeatable for the next few years. Duke's role in the development of the ultra-stable Norton Featherbed frame enabled him to advise Gilera on how to make a similar sort of improvement to the Italian machine, and the Norton-like design of the twin-loop Gilera frame was a testament to his influence, enabling an output of 70bhp at 10,500rpm from the long-stroke 52x58.8mm engine to be successfully harnessed. Only later were the advantages of a higher-revving oversquare engine with more power at the top end to become apparent, and with its two-valve design, 90-degree valve angle and steeply-domed pistons, as well as the four-speed gearbox employed initially (a five-speeder was fitted for the '57 season, and a seven-speed 'box experimented with also), the Gilera was

Blast from the past.

a true child of the '50s. Remor's design set the pattern for subsequent imitation, with central gear drive between the four individually cast alloy cylinders to the twin overhead camshafts, set in a one-piece cylinder head. Unlike the dry-sump Rondine, the postwar Gilera four had a long, finned sump cast integrally with the lower crankcase half of the horizontally-split engine – another advanced feature. The gearbox casing was incorporated in this, with an aluminium upper crankcase. Various size carburettors were fitted depending on track conditions, but two pairs of 28mm Dell'Ortos were commonly used, which in spite of the four megaphone exhausts gave a flexible powerband from 6200rpm upwards, with notable torque compared to later, higher-revving fours.

Fitted with Gilera's own brakes and suspension, the title-winning machines employed a gradually evolving form of full streamlining, culminating in the all-enclosing 'dustbin' fairing of 1957, which improved top speed to almost 170mph. But at the same time as Gilera retired from racing, this form of bodywork was banned by the FIM, so that when the bikes returned to the GP fray under the semi-private Scuderia Duke banner in 1963, ridden by Hartle, Minter and Read, they were fitted with the modern-style 'dolphin' fairings which reduced air penetration but permitted a slight weight reduction: in this final form the Gilera four scaled 149kg without fuel. But time had not stood still, and though Minter especially put in some sterling performances, matched a couple of seasons later by the dramatic efforts of the diminutive Argentinian Benedicto Caldarella in what was to be Gilera's swan song in GP racing, the now-dominant MVs were able to shrug off this born-again challenge from their old rivals. Perhaps Remor had the last laugh, after all.

GILERA 500 FOUR

Engine: Dohc air-cooled transverse in-line four-cylinder four-stroke

Dimensions: 52x58.8mm

Capacity: 499cc

Output: 70bhp at 10,400rpm

Carburation: 4x28mm Dell'Orto

Ignition: Lucas magneto

Gearbox: 7-speed with gear primary

Clutch: Multiplate oilbath

Chassis: Steel tubular duplex cradle

Suspension:
Front: 34mm Gilera telescopic forks
Rear: Steel tubular swingarm with twin Girling units

Brakes:
Front: 250mm four leading-shoe Gilera drum
Rear: 220mm twin leading-shoe Gilera drum

Weight: 149kg

Top speed: 162mph

Year of construction: 1957

AJS 7R3A

Joint owner Jeff Elghanayan speeds the works AJS round the Daytona infield in a latter day vintage race.

7R3A

The introduction of the 350cc AJS 7R single late in 1948, with its chain-driven ohc, telescopic forks, gold-painted magnesium castings and megaphone exhaust of awe-inspiring dimension, marked the first appearance of a machine which would go down in history as one of the all-time great racing motorcycle designs. Over the next two decades, until the late '60s, the 7R (or 'Boys' Racer', as it was initially christened) packed 350 grids and won literally thousands of races all over the world, at all levels and on all types of circuits. In due course, it was scaled up into the 500cc G50 Matchless, which achieved a similar degree of success and together with the Manx Norton came to epitomize the classic British single-cylinder racer.

Fuel was carried low in a large semi-pannier tank.

But strangely enough the AMC factory, owners of the AJS marque, seemed to regard the 7R as a machine destined principally for the use of their customers. They declined to adopt it more than half-heartedly for their works racing team which, though winning the first-ever 500cc world championship in 1949 with Les Graham on the E90 'Porcupine' twin, struggled to attain the same level of success in ensuing seasons in the 500cc class towards which their efforts were directed. Bill Doran's victory in the 1950 Dutch 350 TT on a 7R was the team's only reward for a lack-lustre effort with the original two-valve design.

Low build and bulky cambox are evident here.

Late in 1951 the veteran designer Ike Hatch joined the team and produced one of the most unusual engines ever built to power AJS's 350cc GP class contender in the 1952 season. Popularly known as the 'triple-knocker', this new AJS differed from the standard 74x81mm 7R of the time by incorporating a new shorter-stroke configuration of 75.5x78mm and a three-valve cylinder head, each valve having its own camshaft. The 7R3A, as the new design was officially known, was supposedly a revamped version of the customer machine, but in reality it was a completely new motorcycle, having little in common with the 7R production racer.

In creating the 7R3A, Hatch had several aims: to improve combustion on the relatively low-octane fuel then available; to improve heat conductivity and cool the top half of the engine better; to lessen the chance of valve-spring breakage (always a problem with the materials of the time); and to reduce valve inertia, and thus minimize the risk of

AJS 7R3A

valve float at high rpm. If these targets could be generally grouped under the heading of improving reliability, there was also a chance to gain an improvement in performance by the use of fiercer cam profiles, higher compression, and more revs. Faced with these criteria, Hatch's unique format for the 7R3A – curious by today's standards – becomes more understandable, for the three-valve cylinder head had a single inlet valve, but twin exhaust valves. This is exactly the opposite of modern practice, when designers take fuel quality and metal specification for granted, and are more concerned about filling the combustion chamber as quickly and fully as possible, rather than speedy extraction of the burnt exhaust gases. But burnt exhaust valves and broken springs were a constant headache in Hatch's day, hence the paired exhaust valves of the 7R3A, set radially in the head with a single large inlet, fed by a single $1\,^{3}/_{32}$ inch Amal carburettor. This permitted central location of the single spark plug, thus aiding combustion, while the use of two smaller exhaust valves fitted with triple coil springs, reduced the risk of valve float at the higher rpm of which the new engine was capable – 7500rpm in the gears, against the 7000rpm of the standard 7R. To improve cooling, the exhaust ports were splayed. The chain camshaft drive of the 7R was retained but redirected to drive the rear inlet camshaft directly. This in turn drove a parallel layshaft positioned forward of it, via spur gears, from which the two exhaust valves were disposed at 90° and driven by bevel gears.

A single Amal carburettor is fitted.

The 7R3A engine was used by the AJS works team for three seasons up to and including 1954, their last year of existence before the AMC factory withdrew from racing, in which the Hatch-designed machine scored its only GP victory in the hands of New Zealander Rod Coleman in the Isle of Man Junior TT, with team-mate Derek Farrant second on a similar bike. At the end of the year, as a final flourish, the 7R3A took 13 world 350cc records at Montlhery in France, with a team of riders led by Rod Coleman. Sadly, Hatch died during the course of the year, but not before designing a further version of the AJS 'triple-knocker', the 7R3B, which jettisoned the trademark 7R chain camshaft drive in favour of shaft drive to the rear, inlet camshaft, employing Oldham couplings and bevel gears throughout. Though the new design was track-tested before AJS withdrew, it never raced – but it did mean that by the end of 1954 AMC were running factory bikes with no less than four different means of valve-gear operation: chain-driven ohc (7R/7R3A), shaft-driven ohc (7R3B), gear-driven ohc (E95 'Porcupine' 500) and pushrod ohv (Matchless G45). Quite a full house!

AJS 7R3A

Engine: Triple ohc air-cooled single-cylinder four-stroke

Dimensions: 75.5x78mm

Capacity: 349cc

Output: 42bhp at 8000rpm

Carburation: 1x1⅜ inch Amal GP

Ignition: Lucas magneto

Gearbox: 4-speed with chain primary

Clutch: Multiplate dry

Chassis: Tubular steel duplex with single top tube

Suspension:
Front: AMC telescopic forks
Rear: Tubular steel swingarm with twin AMC units

Brakes:
Front: 8.25 inch twin leading-shoe AMC drum
Rear: 8.25 inch single leading-shoe AMC drum

Weight: 130kg

Top speed: 120mph

Year of construction: 1954

NSU RENNMAX R

This Reynolds-framed Rennmax was built for Geoff Duke to race in 1958, and is now owned by former World TT F3 champion John Kidson.

22

RENNMAX R22

Total domination of your chosen class is always the ultimate aim of every manufacturer entering Grand Prix racing, but for most it remains merely a pipe-dream. Occasionally, though, complete mastery of the opposition is attained, and like the TZ750 Yamaha in the '70s and the 125 Garelli in the '80s, NSU'S 250 Rennmax twin achieved just that in the early 1950s. By general consent one of the evolutionary landmarks of racing motorcycle design – it was the first twin-cylinder 250 four-stroke to make its mark on the GP scene – the Rennmax swept all before it in its brief competition career, both in its original 1952/3 form with twin-bevel shaft cam drive and later 1954 single-shaft guise. NSU won 10 out of 12 GPs contested in 1953/4, took the world title both years, and in doing so made a triumphant return to the international scene that they had been prevented from rejoining by the FIM's postwar ban on GP participation by the German factories, until this was rescinded in 1950.

Reynolds spine frame complements twin-cylinder NSU engine.

After the ban was lifted, NSU's original intention had been to contest the 500cc class with an Italianate in-line dohc four, whose unreliability and uncertain handling as displayed in German national races in 1951 made them think better of the idea. But out of this disaster was born the sweeping success enjoyed by the 250 Rennmax twin and its single-cylinder 125cc Rennfox sister, for both were inspired by the 500 four, though each was essentially different in design, and the product of different engineers, Albert Roder (creator of the 500 and 125) and Walter Froede, the man behind the Rennmax. To create the Rennmax, Froede took two of the 500's 54x54mm cylinders, fitted them on the unit-construction crankcase for a prototype 250 road bike, with four-speed gearbox and single-row chain primary, and added the camshaft drive off NSU's prewar supercharged 350/500 twin, with twin splayed bevel shafts. To this marriage of existing NSU design features he added his own talents for painstaking development, as well as original aspects like the massive, square-finned dohc cylinder head which dominated the engine, fed by a pair of 22mm Fischer-Amal carbs, later increased to 24mm or 25mm depending on the

Dry clutch mates to five-speed gearbox.

NSU RENNMAX R22

type of circuit.

In this form, the Rennmax made its debut in German events during 1952, scoring its first victory in the hands of British ace Bill Lomas at Hamburg in August. Runner-up that day was team-mate Werner Haas, the brilliant young German star who would go on to win both NSU's 250cc world titles

Bristling with ingenuity.

on the machine. It was Haas who gave the bike its foreign debut at Monza the following month, failing by only half a wheel to wrest victory from Lorenzetti's works Guzzi single on the line after a slipstreaming duel. Encouraged by this, Froede redesigned the engine over the winter to incorporate a gear primary, but rather surprisingly placed the result in a heavy pressed-steel backbone frame rather than the original tubular chassis. This gave extra stiffness, desirable in view of the 31bhp now available, at 10,400rpm, and the 18-inch wheels with massive 260mm front brake, and enabled Haas to win the 1953 world 250cc title with new team-mate Reg Armstrong runner-up; between them, the NSU riders won four GP races to defeat the Moto Guzzi reigning champions.

Midway through the season, Froede had introduced a revised version of the Rennmax engine in local German events, which solved the problem NSU experienced of crankshaft whip at five-figure engine speeds with the existing three-bearing pressed-up component, by substituting a five-piece design bolted together by Hirth couplings employing differentially-threaded bolts and

The NSU engine is as complex as a watch mechanism.

Twin overhead camshafts are driven by splined bevels of the left end of the crankshaft.

NSU RENNMAX R22

radially-serrated mating faces. This expensive and complicated but very strong method completely eliminated the problem, and for 1954 Froede totally redesigned the Rennmax engine to incorporate it in a new short-stroke 55.9x50.88mm configuration with four-bearing crank permitting higher revs and thus more power. This now had a simplified camshaft drive with a single vertical shaft located behind the cylinders, driving the separate camshafts - one for each valve, with each pair joined by Oldham couplings - by means of a trio of spur gears. With huge 40mm inlet valves, an advanced included valve angle of only 50 degrees, and a six-speed gearbox, the NSU Rennmax now delivered a remarkable 39bhp at 11,500rpm and scaled only 135kg, even when fitted with the firm's distinctive bluff-fronted alloy streamlining, in which form it had a tcp speed of more than 135mph. This not only made it more than a match for any other 250, but the equal of existing 350s and single-cylinder 500s: by contrast, the world champion 350 Guzzi single had the same 39bhp output as the 250 Rennmax, while a stroked 288cc version which Froede produced 'just to see' yielded 40.4bhp at 11,200rpm.

But NSU's threatened onslaught on the 350 class never happened. Instead, after completely dominating the 250cc category in 1954, winning all 24 races which they contested, including all seven GPs, they retired from the fray in order to concentrate on their road bike production and future plans for a car range. Haas had won the first five GPs in a row on the new bike, which scored a crushing 1-2-3-4 win on its GP debut at Reims, but his team-mate Rupert Hollaus - already crowned 125 world champion on the Rennfox - was killed in a practice crash at the last race of the year at Monza. This sour end to the NUS team's championship season was also their farewell from racing, for they were not seen in motorcycle racing again. A joint effort by Reg Armstrong and Geoff Duke to race a Reynolds-framed Rennmax with an engine supplied by the factory in '58 proved unsuccessful, and though the single-cylinder Sportmax proved a successful privateer mount throughout the rest of the decade (also winning 'Happy' Muller the world title in 1955), the Rennmax was seen no more: it had come, seen, conquered - and departed.

John Kidson and his NSU.

NSU RENNMAX R22

Engine: Dohc air-cooled parallel twin-cylinder four-stroke

Dimensions: 54x54mm

Capacity: 247cc

Output: 31bhp at 10,400rpm

Carburation: 2x26mm Fischer-Amal GP

Ignition: 6v battery/coil

Gearbox: 4-speed with gear primary

Clutch: Multiplate dry

Chassis: Tubular steel backbone with duplex cradle

Suspension:
Front: Reynolds fabricated leading-link telescopic forks with Armstrong damper units
Rear: Steel tubular swingarm with twin Girling units

Brakes:
Front: 260mm full-width single leading-shoe NSU drum
Rear: 190mm single leading-shoe NSU drum

Weight: 122kg

Top speed: 120mph

Year of construction: 1959

MOTO GUZZI

350 BIALBER

Twice world 350cc champion in 1955–56 on the Guzzi single, Bill Lomas demonstrates the 1956 title-winner at a Salzburgring Oldtimer GP meeting.

O

350 BIALBERO

Undefeated champion of the 350cc class during the 1950s.

Though the more exotic 500 Bicilindrica V-twin, the in-line four and the fabulous V8 all received more attention both at the time they were raced and since, all Moto Guzzi's eight world titles won between 1949, when the world championships began, and 1957, when the Italian company pulled out of racing, were acquired by their less complex but no less remarkable single-cylinder machines. It wasn't so much that the Guzzi single succeeded in withstanding the challenge of the Gilera and MV fours so emphatically, nor even that its success marked the end of the Manx Norton's reign both as champion of the world and supreme single: it was the way in which it did so. Out of 35 350cc GP races during the 1953–7 era, no fewer than 24 were won by the Mandello marvels, a degree of opposition which is all the more remarkable when the calibre of the combined opposition is taken into account. And in producing the ultimate version of the 350 Bialbero for 1957, after which Guzzi announced their shock retirement from racing together with Gilera and Mondial, designer Giulio Carcano constructed a machine which, in weighing a scant 98kg, broke the 100kg barrier for the 350 class for the first time. And in spite of an output of just 38bhp, this machine was capable of a top speed of no less than 146mph, due to the highly effective 'dustbin' streamlining developed in the factory's own wind tunnel.

Typical Guzzi rider's 'office'.

One reason for the Guzzi's light build was that in creating the 350 Bialbero, Carcano followed the first rule of GP development and scaled up rather than down, though he did try it the other way first. Guzzi's first participation in the 350 class, which the Italians traditionally regarded as the private territory of the British manufacturers, took place in 1949 when they tried to pose some sort of threat to Norton, AJS and Velocette by sleeving down one of the wide-angle 120-degree 500cc V-twins. The result was far too heavy, but early in 1953 Carcano tried again from the other direction by producing a twin-cam, oversize version of the successful 250 Gambalunghino, measuring 72x79mm for 317cc, in which form it developed just 31bhp at 7700rpm; the 250 works racer it was derived from measured 68x72mm. In this form, the 350 Guzzi Bialbero won its first-ever race in the hands of Fergus Anderson, the German GP on the ultra-fast German track. This surprise debut victory convinced the hitherto

The single that beat the fours.

MOTO GUZZI 350 B

The large fuel tank sat deep inside the spaceframe chassis.

ALBERO

sceptical Carcano to redesign the engine completely to make a full 350 with his preferred dimensions of 75x78mm (for 345cc), later to be stroked 1mm further to give 349cc. Thereafter, Anderson won three of the last five GP races in the '53 season, to give Guzzi their first of five successive world titles in the class.

For 1954, the 350 Guzzi was completely redesigned after the mid-season rush job the previous year, with a heavily oversquare 80x69.5mm engine, delivering 35bhp at 7800rpm. The design followed established Guzzi works single practice, with a deeply-finned horizontal cylinder fitted with a dohc cylinder head, and shaft and bevel drive to the cams, but enclosed coil springs were now fitted instead of the exposed hairpin valve springs, and dual ignition with a battery and coils replaced the traditional Guzzi magneto. A three-piece crank shaft with Hirth couplings, permitting a solid conrod, replaced the old one-piece crank, and specially-made Dell'Orto carbs in a variety of choke sizes from 35mm up to, eventually, a massive 45mm depending on the circuit, were fitted in a down-draught position. The chassis, too, had been completely revised, with the so-called 'Bailey Bridge' design, a multi-tube triangulated spaceframe with the fuel carried in a cylindrical tank above the cylinder. This took full advantage of the horizontal single's low build, especially when coupled with new wind tunnel-designed streamlining which yielded a top speed of 220kph – compared to the first overbored 250's mere 190kph.

The new machine suffered inevitable teething troubles, but all was resolved in time for Anderson to win his second world title, culminating in leading a 1–4 Guzzi sweep in front of ecstatic crowds in the Italian GP at Monza. For 1955 it remained largely unchanged, though fuel was now carried in two separate pannier tanks on either side of the engine, pumped up mechanically to a header tank, from which the carb was fed. Weight was reduced slightly to 122kg by eliminating the rear wheel fairing, and in this guise the Guzzi won every 350cc GP that year, with Lomas the champion after four wins and another 1–4 clean sweep at Monza. The next

Later 500cc single was externally all but identical to the 350 it sprang from.

MOTO GUZZI 350 B

year Carcano met the challenge of the new four-cylinder MV by designing a new frame with large-diameter spine tube, which doubled as an oil tank and from which the engine was suspended. The streamlining had become more graceful and well-rounded, and even more effective, and with a slight power increase Lomas took his second world title and Guzzi's fourth. For 1957, Carcano revamped the engine back to 75x79mm longstroke dimensions to regain lost torque and flexibility, thus making the bikes more ridable. Every possible means was followed to reduce weight, resulting in a machine which, while only just outpaced by the fours on top speed, had a distinct advantage on acceleration thanks to its scant weight. Guzzi's new Australian recruit, Keith Campbell, won three GPs to take the title, while had it not been for Guzzi's ensuing retirement from the sport, the new 500 Bialbero Carcano had produced for the 1955 season, based closely on the 350 but measuring 88x82mm, in which form it produced 42bhp at 7000rpm and took Bill Lomas to victory in the Ulster GP that year, would perhaps have emulated the success of its smaller sister in the 500 class. The Moto Guzzi singles' unique combination of light weight, low centre of gravity, fuel economy,

'Dustbin' fairing helped top speed performance.

effective air penetration, high specific power and, above all, reliability, made them a powerful and successful weapon on every type of circuit in the 1950s. They were the two-wheeled embodiment of the dictum that 'less is more'.

It could only be a Guzzi!

MOTO GUZZI 350 BIALBERO

Engine: Dohc air-cooled single-cylinder four-stroke

Dimensions: 75x79mm

Capacity: 349cc

Output: 38bhp at 7800rpm

Carburation: 1x45mm Dell'Orto

Ignition: 6v battery/coil, with twin plugs

Gearbox: 5-speed with gear primary

Clutch: Multiplate oilbath

Chassis: Tubular spine with triangulated subframes

Suspension:
Front: Moto Guzzi leading-link telescopic forks with remote springs
Rear: Tubular swingarm with twin Marzocchi units

Brakes:
Front: 230mm twin leading-shoe Moto Guzzi drum
Rear: 210mm single leading-shoe Moto Guzzi drum

Weight: 99kg

Top speed: 142mph

Year of construction: 1957

ALBERO

GILERA

125 BICILIND

The Gilera factory's museum piece receives an outing at Monza in a historic race meeting.

RICA

125 BICILINDRICA

Unlike most of their Italian counterparts, Gilera had never contested the small-capacity classes, preferring to concentrate on the blue riband 500cc category. But the introduction of their 150cc ohv roadster in the early '50s meant that Italy's oldest bike manufacturer was now in competition for lightweight street bike sales with the new generation of marques like Mondial and MV. Almost inevitably, this being Italy, that meant expanding the arena for this commercial conflict to include not only the showroom, but also the track.

In 1954 Gilera designer Franco Passoni began work on a radical new 125cc racer which eventually made its debut at the start of the 1956 season, scoring a brilliant victory on the ultra-fast Monza track in the hands of Romolo Ferri, who defeated reigning world champion Carlo Ubbiali's MV Agusta on home ground. But in designing the little Gilera racer, Passoni had resisted the obvious temptation simply to slice one cylinder off the company's all-conquering 500cc four; instead he produced the first twin-cylinder four-stroke to be raced in the 125cc GP class. In this sense, therefore, the Gilera Bicilindrica represented the start of the trend towards ever greater miniaturization which would become a key aspect of GP racing over the next decade, leading to such mechanical marvels as the five-cylinder 125cc Honda and the three-

Unit construction engine bears factory hallmark.

GILERA 125 BICILIN

Low, clean and neat – the first 125cc GP twin.

cylinder 50cc Suzuki. In the short term, though the Gilera was a harbinger of the works Honda twins that would come to dominate the 125 class half a decade later (and lead to one of the best-loved production racers of all time, the CR93), which for all their Oriental mystique were closely based on the specification of the Italian bike.

This predicated a 360-degree parallel-twin, with the cylinders inclined forward 30 degrees from vertical, air-cooled and with double overhead camshafts gear-driven up the centre of the engine off the crank. But unlike the Honda, the Gilera had only two valves per cylinder, and moreover followed its four-cylinder cousin in having, by multi-cylinder standards, a curious long-stroke configuration of 40x49.6mm. The aim was obviously to go for torque rather than high revs and a narrow powerband, but in spite of this the little Italian twin revved to 12,000rpm, at which point it delivered 19bhp, with power from 8000 onwards – not a bad

Dolphin-type fairing.

degree of flexibility, especially by later standards. Coil ignition was employed for the first time on a Gilera racer, since Passoni was not convinced of a magneto's ability to keep up with these high revs, with two 25mm Dell'Orto carburettors. The unit-construction engine followed traditional Italian practice in having wet-sump lubrication, but at a time when its 125cc rivals had five or even four-speed gearboxes, the Gilera had a six-speeder.

This jewel-like little power unit was fitted in a conventional twin-loop open-cradle frame which in early tests appeared with leading-link forks, though these were replaced by telescopics by the time the bike first raced. A long, slim fuel tank was partially

Compact build of twin-cylinder engine is evident here.

sunk between the upper frame rails, leading to a very low, stretched-out riding position which enabled the diminutive Ferri to tuck himself away within the all-enveloping streamlining. This was the key to the little Gilera's amazing turn of speed, only a whisker short of the magic 200kph barrier for the 125cc class. However, the full-enclosure bodywork also made engine cooling critical, and in the bike's first GP at Spa in 1956, Ferri retired with overheating after setting a new lap record of more than 100mph – the first time this mark had been beaten in a 125 GP race. Team-mate Pierre Monneret finished third on this occasion, but in the next race at the Solitudering in Germany, the Gilera reappeared with modified cooling ducts, and Ferri scored his and the bike's first world championship race win. In the next race, making his first visit to Ulster and the tricky Dundrod circuit, he finished second to Ubbiali's MV single, while a retirement with piston trouble in front of the home crowd at Monza in the Italian GP brought bitter disappointment, only partially compensated for by a final victory in the non-title Swedish GP at Hedemora.

Skinny tyres helped maximise top speed.

GILERA 125 BICILIN

Ferri had finished second to Ubbiali's MV in the '56 world championship, an encouraging debut for the Gilera twin which the company took full advantage of in terms of publicity. The team began the 1957 season with high hopes for the title, which in spite of two defeats by Provini on the suddenly competitive dohc Mondial single in early-season Italian races, seemed more than reasonable. But then Romolo Ferri, with whom the 125 GP project had been so closely linked, crashed in the next race and was badly injured, putting himself *hors de combat* for the rest of the season. Under pressure from MV in the 500cc class they had made their own, and with the new 350 four attempting to overturn Guzzi domination of that class, too, Gilera decided it was not worth starting afresh with a new rider in the 125 category. At the end of the season, with Ferri recovered from his injuries, the little bike took a series of 125cc world records at Monza, including the hour mark at no less than 197.774kph.

Gilera's withdrawal from racing at the end of '57 meant that the 125 twin never fulfilled its true potential, and though the two bikes built were dug out of the factory museum, and fitted with modern-type bodywork for Masserini and Lombardi to run in the 1967 Italian championship, the world had passed them by. But, 10 years beforehand, the smallest Gilera racer had pointed small-capacity GP race development in an exciting new direction.

Dohc twin is small-scale relation of Gilera's 500 four.

Rear camshaft drove points ignition.

GILERA 125 BICILINDRICA

Engine: Dohc air-cooled parallel twin-cylinder four-stroke

Dimensions: 40x49.6mm

Capacity: 124cc

Output: 19bhp at 12,000rpm

Carburation: 2x25mm Dell'Orto

Ignition: 6v battery/coil

Gearbox: 6-speed with gear primary

Clutch: Multiplate oilbath

Chassis: Tubular steel duplex cradle

Suspension:
Front: 30mm Gilera telescopic forks
Rear: Steel tubular swingarm with twin Koni units

Brakes:
Front: 200mm twin leading-shoe Gilera drum
Rear: 190mm single leading-shoe Gilera drum

Weight: 105kg

Top speed: 120mph

Year of construction: 1956

ORICA

DKW
350 THREE-C

Wafting along in the wind: the streamlined DKW at speed.

YLINDER

350 THREE-CYLINDER

Alone of major factories before World War II, the German DKW marque's perseverance in the cause of two-stroke racing development was eventually rewarded by domination of the 250 and 350cc classes with their noisy, exceedingly thirsty, but phenomenally fast supercharged, water-cooled split-singles. But with the postwar ban on forced induction, DKW's new generation of engineers had to start afresh – a difficulty compounded by the division of Germany, which left the DKW motorcycle factory at Zschopau on the wrong side of the barbed wire. In due course, renamed MZ, this concern would play a major role in the development of the modern two-stroke racing engine, thanks to the genius of Walter Kaaden's rotary-valve designs. But before that, the born-again DKW marque, re-established postwar on the western side of the Iron Curtain in Ingolstadt, would play a similarly important role in the two-stroke's rise to GP power.

DKW were one of the first to adopt full-enclosure streamlining in the mid-50s.

Massive ATE brakes have hydraulic actuation.

With the readmission of Germany to international competition for the 1951 season, the way was open for DKW's designers to grapple with the problems of making an unsupercharged two-stroke competitive with four-strokes. This they did, to brilliant effect, but not overnight. First came a single-cylinder 125cc machine, with a cylindrical rotary valve placed crossways behind the cylinder and gear-driven off the crank. A 250 twin was obtained by simply doubling up the design, and after the valve was relocated running lengthways between the cylinders, the resultant output of 22bhp was sufficient to give riders Gustl Höbl and veteran Siggi Wünsche a pair of third places in the Isle of Man TT and the German GP. But at this stage, the DKWs were no match for the all-conquering four-stroke NSU Rennmax twins.

At the end of that season, the 250 DKW twin was transformed into a 350 triple by replacing the forward-facing magneto located at the front end of the rotary valve with a third cylinder, now measuring 53x52.8mm instead of the 250's 54x54mm. With the two outer cylinders inclined forwards 15 degrees to aid cooling, fitting the horizontal third cylinder should have resulted in high-frequency vibrations from the consequent 75-degree included cylinder angle – as Honda were to discover three decades later with their NS500 triple, which adopted the same format. But DKW solved this problem and obtained the desired 120-degree firing interval by using offset crankpins, a feature rediscovered by the Japanese for four-stroke use

Large hand-beaten alloy fuel tank.

DKW 350 THREE-C

Fabricated leading-link forks are fitted.

in the 1980s. DKW also reverted on the 350 to piston-port induction, with a single 28mm Dell'Orto carburettor per cylinder, and now placed the Bosch magneto – designed for the BMW 328 six-cylinder sports car – on the right of the crankcase, driven by a spur gear off the crank itself. A five-speed gearbox with gear primary drive was fitted. The DKW's initial output of 31bhp was inadequate to be competitive, and though development continued, Höbl's fourth place in the '53 Italian GP was the early bike's best result. But a mid-season shake-up in the racing department during 1954 saw the appointment of a brilliant young engineer, Helmut Görg, to oversee the 350 project, and after he completely revamped the design for the 1954 season, DKW at last found the renewed success they had hoped for.

Flat-sided exhaust boxes.

Görg's genius may be gauged by the fact that in little more than two years he increased the power of the DKW engine from 35bhp at 10,000rpm when he took over, to 45bhp at 9700rpm by the time the factory retired from racing at the end of the 1956 season. By this time the triple had been fitted with all-enveloping streamlining developed in the Munich Technical College's wind tunnel, which enabled it to reach a top speed of 230kph on the banked Avus track in Berlin. Moreover, the chassis had been revamped into a sturdy duplex frame with single top tube and fabricated rear bulkhead which, fitted with leading-link forks and massive ATE hydraulically-operated drum brakes, enabled

LINDER

Huge cooling scoops dominate front brake: but where did the hot air escape?

DKW 350 THREE-CY

riders Höbl, Hoffmann and Briton Cecil Sandford to make good use of the engine's potential. Only one Achilles' heel remained: time after time, the flying DKWs would blast off into the lead of a race, only to fade as the race progressed and the engine overheated and lost power. Water-cooling would have been the solution, but Görg was never able to get corporate approval for this step:.

V3 design permitted compact engine dimensions.

Despite this one drawback, the revitalized DKW three-cylinder took August Höbl to third place in the 1955 world 350cc championship, and equal second the following season. Sadly, the bike never won a single Grand Prix race, thanks mainly to the brilliance of Bill Lomas, the Moto Guzzi single and another great engineer, Giulio Carcano. But DKW had the last laugh, for when Freddie Spencer won Honda's first-ever world 500cc crown in 1983, it was with a modern version of the V3 DKW two-stroke: nothing new under the Rising Sun!

Simple but effective spine frame is clearly shown.

DKW 350 THREE-CYLINDER

Engine: Air-cooled piston-port 75-degree V3 two-stroke

Dimensions: 53x52.8mm

Capacity: 349cc

Output: 45bhp at 9700rpm

Carburation: 3x28mm Dell'Orto

Ignition: 6v battery/coil

Gearbox: 5-speed with gear primary

Clutch: Multiplate dry

Chassis: Tubular steel duplex cradle with single top tube and fabricated bulkhead

Suspension:
Front: Fabricated steel leading-link forks with twin Stabilus units
Rear: Tubular steel swingarm with twin Girling units

Brakes:
Front: 210mm four leading-shoe ATE drum with linked hydraulic operation and auxiliary cable system
Rear: 210mm four leading-shoe ATE drum with hydraulic operation

Weight: 147kg

Top speed: 143mph

Year of construction: 1955

LINDER

DUCATI 125 DESMO

Ducati handling was adequate rather than exceptional: the engine's the thing.

DUCATI

125 DESMO

The principle of positive valve control, or desmodromics, whereby the valve is opened *and* closed by mechanical means, without use of springs, was well known in the car world by the time Italian designer Fabio Taglioni joined the rapidly expanding Ducati motorcycle factory in Bologna in 1954. The Mercedes-Benz cars which dominated that year's world motor-racing F1 championship were fitted with straight-eight desmo engines, and there had been several experiments with various forms of desmodromics right back to the dawn of the internal combustion engine.

Taglioni was the first to develop the idea for two-wheeled use on a viable basis, first in his racing designs, then later, in a brave commercial risk (given the fine engineering tolerances required), in the range of Ducati street bikes sold to their customers. The gamble paid off to such an extent that, decades later, the words Ducati and desmo are unfailingly linked in the mind of the motorcycle enthusiast. Today, the Italian factory remains the only marque in the world to sell (and race) a desmo motorcycle.

Taglioni's arrival at Ducati from the rival Mondial marque (where he had already experimented with a desmo prototype) led immediately to the development of a range of sporting lightweights based on his first design for the company, the single overhead-cam 98cc Gran Sport, affectionately known by all and sundry as the 'Marianna'. This provided the format on which all future Ducati singles, both road and race, were based, with an air-cooled cylinder inclined forward 10 degrees from vertical,

Desmo engine uses same bottom end design as other Ducati singles.

DUCATI 125 DESMO

unit-construction with gear primary drive, wet-sump lubrication, battery ignition, and camshaft drive by vertical shaft and bevels. In light of Taglioni's passionate belief in testing all his designs in competition before developing them for road use, it was no surprise that the Marianna came to dominate its class in Italian national racing, first in the hands of the works team, then later its customers.

The next step was to produce a dohc 125cc version of the Gran Sport, which – still employing hairpin valve springs in the two-valve head – appeared for the 1956 season in the hands of a factory team comprising no less than 14 riders! But the high rpm at which the engine needed to operate to produce competitive power led to problems with valve float which Taglioni believed could only be overcome with a desmodromic cylinder head.

Amadoro brakes were light but effective.

1958 chassis used single downrube with bifurcated cradle.

Slim single was originally fitted with dustbin fairing before 1958 rule change.

This was achieved by replacing the twin-cam cylinder head with a new triple-camshaft design, still retaining the Marianna-derived bottom end with its bevel gear and shaft camshaft drive. This drove the middle of the three camshafts, on which both closing cams were located, with the outer two camshafts each bearing a single, opening, lobe; all operated the valves by means of forked rockers. The degree of accuracy needed to obtain the required tolerances was considerable, representing a major technical feat for a small factory like Ducati in the days before computer-aided manufacture. The desmo cylinder head was a true work of metallurgical art, both cambox and head being cast as one unit in light alloy, though the rest of the 55.3x52mm engine, which naturally measured the same as the valve-spring twin-cam Grand Prix model it was descended from, was relatively conventional by Italian lightweight standards, and closely followed the Marianna design. But instead of the four-speed gearbox fitted previously, a five-speed unit was now employed, mated to an oil-bath clutch, with the extra ratio fitted outside the crankcase wall behind the clutch. A 29mm Dell'Orto carburettor was employed for fast circuits (a smaller choke size for twistier ones), and the net result was to raise both revs and power output dramatically: whereas the 125 Grand Prix yielded 16bhp at 11,500rpm, and could not be revved higher without breaking a valve spring or succumbing to valve float, the desmo yielded 19bhp at 12,500rpm, with the engine safe on the overrun to an amazing 15,000rpm – though inevitably big-end life was very short at these sort of speeds, and new crankshaft bearings were fitted for every race.

The 125 desmo Ducati first raced at the 1956 Swedish GP at Hedemora, winning so convincingly in the hands of works tester Gianni degli Antoni that he lapped every other finisher. But he was tragi-

DUCATI 125 DESMO

cally killed practising for the next race, the Italian GP, at Monza, and this setback, combined with reliability problems with the new design, meant that it was not until 1958 that Ducati was able to challenge the established might of MV Agusta and former champion Carlo Ubbiali in the 125cc GPs.

But in this season, with a top-line team of riders well equipped to extract the maximum from Taglioni's little jewel, Ducati all but clinched their first world title, with Alberto Gandossi, Romolo Ferri, Luigi Taveri, Bruno Spaggiari, Dave Chadwick and Sammy Miller all variously mounted on the desmo singles. Ducatis won in Belgium, Sweden and Italy, the latter a triumphal sweep of the first five places in their home GP which sent the rival MV team home despondent, even though a mid-season injury to team leader Spaggiari had permitted MV's Ubbiali narrowly to regain his title, in spite of being outpaced.

Desmo valve gear.

Ducati had made their point, though: in spite of failing to attain their world title goal, they had proved that desmodromics worked, not only as a means of extracting more power from the engine via higher revs, but also as a useful safety factor in the event of a missed gear – something that generations of customers would come to appreciate in later years.

In 1959 they downgraded their GP effort, with a new rider named Mike Hailwood winning the Dutch GP on a 125 desmo to register Ducati's only GP win that season before the factory retired from racing to concentrate on developing a new range of road bikes. Eight years later, the first desmo Ducati road bikes were put on sale, living proof of the maxim that racing really does improve the breed.

DUCATI 125 DESMO

Engine: Triple-camshaft air-cooled desmodromic single-cylinder four-stroke

Dimensions: 55.3x52mm

Capacity: 124cc

Output: 18bhp at 12500rpm

Carburation: 1x27mm Dell'Orto

Ignition: 6v battery/coil

Gearbox: 5-speed with gear primary

Clutch: Multiplate oilbath

Chassis: Tubular steel duplex cradle

Suspension:
Front: 30mm Marzocchi telescopic forks
Rear: Tubular steel swingarm with twin Marzocchi units

Brakes:
Front: 205mm twin leading-shoe Amadoro drum
Rear: 180mm single leading-shoe Amadoro drum

Weight: 81kg

Top speed: 110mph

Year of construction: 1958

MATCHLESS G50

Spanish rider Joaquin Folch on his Matchless G50, complete with period modifications such as high-rise exhaust and Ceriani front brake.

MATCHLESS

G50

For most of the '50s the only alternative to the Manx Norton produced by a British factory for the 500cc class was the pushrod Matchless G45 twin, a fast but unreliable device full of inherent compromises which was no match for the dohc single. Yet in the 350 class,the AMC factory which owned both AJS and Matchless built and sold a substantial number of 7R AJS production racers, which largely eclipsed its 350 Norton rival as the preferred choice of the privateer.

In retrospect, it seems incredible that it should have taken so long for the penny to drop in the collective mind of the AMC board, but at long last in 1958 they finally did the obvious and authorized the head of the racing department, Jack Williams, to proceed with the development of a 500cc version of the 7R. Thus at long last the Manx Norton's only true rival for the role of the ultimate British single-cylinder racer was born: the Matchless G50.

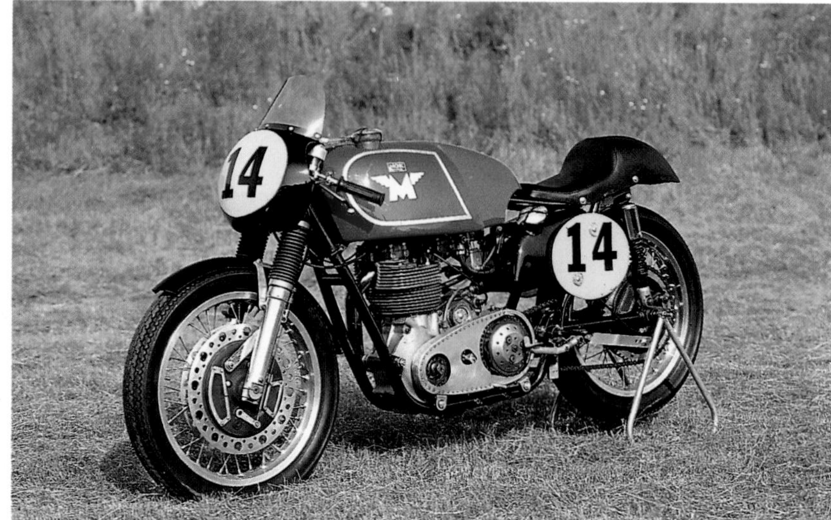

Completely original G50 apart from non-standard 18-inch wheels and modern tyres.

Single-loop chassis.

Given that Williams had already revamped the 7R engine in 1956 to a new shorter-stroke configuration, based on that employed on the works 7R3A model of 75.5x78mm, creating the G50 appeared at first sight to mean little more than 'just' boring out the 7R to 90x78mm for a capacity of 496cc. In fact, that's all Williams initially did, and the first pair of G50 machines built and raced by Jack Ahearne in the Senior TT and John Holder in the Race of the Year were literally overbored 350s with a larger piston and sleeve.

Results were sufficiently encouraging for Williams to be permitted to develop a 'proper' 500, which went into production for the 1959 season. This had the same overall format as the 7R AJS, whose original design was produced by AMC engineer Phil Walker back in 1947, with a two-valve cylinder head employing hairpin springs with full enclosure, and chain-driven single overhead camshaft with a Weller tensioner. Extensive use of magnesium castings meant that the engines were painted a distinctive gold colour to resist corrosion. Chain primary drive mated the roller-bearing crank to a four-speed gearbox, and though the 350cc engine gradually evolved over the years, it retained the same basic design, which also thus spawned the 500cc G50.

The '59 version of the Matchless racer had a revamped cylinder head with larger 1¾ inch exhaust valve and 1⅞ inch inlet, with a large 1½ inch Amal GP carburettor. In this form the engine delivered 51.5bhp at 7200rpm, slightly less than the equivalent Manx Norton, which was thus faster on top speed by around 5mph in standard form.

Twin leading-shoe front brake with cooling ring.

MATCHLESS G50

But at 130kg dry in standard, unfaired form, the G50 was also substantially lighter than the Manx, giving better acceleration which, allied with the more tractable nature of its engine, made it the Manx's measure on twisty circuits. At the same time, it was also easier to work on - the Norton's complex and heavy dohc cylinder head was both a strength and a weakness - and was less expensive to maintain, always a strong point with the perpetually hard-up privateers forming the bulk of GP grids in those days of the Continental Circus.

But the rival Norton was so well established that, initially at least, the G50 found it hard to attract converts - though production problems at AMC meant there was a waiting list in the early days. This encouraged Williams to try to narrow the performance gap with the Manx by introducing a larger, two-inch exhaust valve for 1962, the last year of production for the G50, by which time 180 examples had been built. The result was certainly a little more powerful, but a lot less pleasant to ride since the G50's prime card, its tractability, suffered adversely as a result. It was left to the various AMC

Magnesium covers painted gold to resist corrosion.

Distinctive fuel tank displays deep cutouts for knees.

Camshaft drive is by chain; carb is a large 1 inch Amal GP.

MATCHLESS G50

specialist tuners, mostly unsung former members of the AMC race shop who had set up on their own when it was closed down, to continue development after the end of production in a successful effort to combine the best of both worlds. This explains why it was only some time after production officially ceased that the G50 Matchless really came into its own, empirical development pushing output up to over 55bhp and revs as high as 8000rpm by the mid-'60s.

In 1966, AJS and Matchless's parent company Associated Motor Cycles finally went bankrupt, and the rights to the 7R/G50 were acquired by former sidecar racer Colin Seeley. He continued to manufacture an improved, stronger version of the original motor (with aluminium crankcases), offering the engine either for sale on its own, to update an existing Matchless, for use in a specialist frame like a Rickman Metisse, or as part of a complete bike, the Seeley G50. This was in many ways the ultimate British short circuit special, which also enjoyed great success at GP level well into the 1970s, before slipping back into the club racing world as the relentless march of two-stroke machinery swamped the British singles.

But little more than a decade later, the G50 Matchless was back at the top of its chosen class, this time the blossoming world of Classic racing, which it has dominated almost from its inception thanks to a ready supply of re-manufactured spare parts including, latterly, complete G50 engines. In 1984 the G50 finally won a TT race in the Isle of Man, albeit the first (and, so far, only) Historic TT, ridden by American Dave Roper. After Peter Williams (son of engineer Jack) had four times finished second in the Senior TT between 1967 and 1973, on the specially-framed Arter Matchless, on the final occasion averaging over 100mph to do so, justice was finally done.

Ready for action.

MATCHLESS G50

Engine: Sohc air-cooled single-cylinder four-stroke

Dimensions: 90x78mm

Capacity: 496cc

Output: 51bhp at 7200rpm

Carburation: 1x1½ inch Amal GP

Ignition: Lucas magneto

Gearbox: 4-speed with chain primary

Clutch: Multiplate dry

Chassis: Steel duplex tubular engine cradle with single top tube

Suspension:
Front: AMC telescopic forks
Rear: Tubular steel swingarm with twin Girling units

Brakes:
Front: 8.25 inch twin leading-shoe AMC drum
Rear: 8.25 inch single leading-shoe AMC drum

Weight: 132kg

Top speed: 135mph

Year of construction: 1961

BENELLI 250 FOUR

Twice a world champion on Mondials, Tarquinio Provini was Benelli's first star on the 250 four.

250 FOUR

Benelli were noted for their conservative engineering, by Italian standards, but in June 1960 they astonished the road racing world by unveiling an in-line dohc four-cylinder 250cc racer which had gone from drawing board to test track in the space of just over six months. Its appearance was all the more dramatic given that Benelli's racing activities had lain largely dormant since Ambrosini had clinched the first world title for the Pesaro-based family concern in 1950 on a dohc single, whose design dated from well into the prewar era.

Benelli had already earned the accolade, together with the concurrent Gilera, designing the world's first 250cc four-cylinder racer, a supercharged, water-cooled prototype whose development when it appeared in 1940 was aborted by World War II. The new 250 four was quite different, being an air-cooled design produced jointly by Giovanni Benelli, one of the six brothers who founded the family firm in 1911, and the head of the racing department, Ing. Savesi.

Compact engine employed one piece crankcase casting.

Italian tricolore stripes adorn drab grey fairing.

The new machine was to prove the progenitor of a line of Benelli fours whose development would occupy the greater part of the 1960s, before being rewarded finally with a world 250cc title in 1969 in the hands of Australian Kel Carruthers. Like its successors, this first prototype had the crankcase and gearbox housing combined in one large but very light electron casting, with a large rectangular front cover and four round side covers through which the engine and gearbox internals could be slotted and which meant that the gear cluster could be removed to change the internal ratios without dismantling the rest of the engine. Two of the side covers located the ends of the six-bearing, built-up crankshaft, making for a rigid and oil-tight design which could be quickly rebuilt with a minimum of inconvenience. Though the first prototype featured dry-sump lubrication, by the time the 250 Benelli four made its racing debut in April '62 in the hands of Silvio Grassetti, it had reverted to the 'classical' Italian design with a long, finned, bolt-on sump beneath the engine, and was now fitted with a six-speed gearbox and Lucas magneto, replacing the original points ignition. In this form, the 44x40.6mm engine delivered 45bhp at 14,000rpm, enabling Grassetti to clinch victory in the Benelli's second race at Cesenatico that Italian spring.

But development proceeded slowly, and during 1963 the Benelli four was no match for the remarkable Morini single which came so close to winning the 250cc world title that year. Accordingly, Benelli took the obvious step of hiring the Morini's brave and resourceful rider, Tarquinio Provini, for the '64 season, and under his guidance the machine was

You can almost hear the sound from those four pipes!

BENELLI 250 FOUR

In-line engine is fed by four 24mm Dell'Ortos.

transformed into a truly competitive mount. A new twin-loop chassis with long, slim, 'anatomical' fuel tank not only brought a reduction in weight to only 112kg, but enabled the rider to crouch almost prone beneath the screen, thus maximizing air penetration. Engine modifications raised the rev limit to 14,500rpm, with 48bhp now available, still with two valves per cylinder and single plug ignition. A seven-speed gearbox was now employed, with four 20mm Dell'Orto carburettors. In Provini's hands the Benelli four now became a real contender for top honours, defeating the Japanese works team in the '64 Spanish GP round the twisty Montjuich Park circuit, and easily winning the Italian 250 title. But more power was needed to defeat the Honda fours on faster tracks, so for 1965 further changes were made, with power now up to 52bhp and engine speed to 15,000rpm. The Lucas magneto, designed for car use, was unable to cope with these rpm, and was replaced by one from a Mercury outboard engine, modified for four-stroke use, which solved the problem. Benelli also became one of the first teams to experiment with

Large diameter clutch sits on left of engine.

Short wheelbase gave fast steering.

BENELLI 250 FOUR

disc brakes, fitting a pair of US-made seven-inch Airheart discs originally employed on go-karts to the front, but after problems with wet-weather braking and lack of pad choice, these were shelved in favour of the more usual Ceriani drums. Provini won the Italian GP at Monza in '65, in pouring rain, but still the Benelli was unable to compete with the Japanese at world level on a regular basis. Thus, a 16-valve engine appeared for the 1966 season, which pushed power up to 55bhp and safe revs to 16,000rpm, but though Provini won the Italian title yet again, he crashed in practice for the Isle of Man TT and suffered severe back injuries which ended his racing career.

This setback dented Benelli's hopes for a couple of seasons, while Provini's replacement, the exuberant, bespectacled Renzo Pasolini, found his feet on the smallest Pesaro four. After a series of top three places in the GPs, Pasolini started the '69 season favourite to take the world title but he, too, was injured early in the season, so it was left to privateer Kel Carruthers, hastily drafted into the team for the TT, to win not only on the Isle of Man but also in Ulster and Yugoslavia, to score Benelli's long-awaited second 250cc world championship. It had taken a long decade of development to turn the four-cylinder 250 into a title-winner, but it was only just in time; for the next season, the FIM limited 250cc machines to a maximum of two cylinders and six gearbox speeds, thus overnight rendering one of the most technically interesting European GP machines of the 1960s obsolete. Fortunately, Benelli's persistence and dedication to the sport had by then already been rewarded with the success it merited.

Works mechanic, Censi.

BENELLI 250 FOUR

Engine: Dohc air-cooled transverse in-line four-cylinder four-stroke

Dimensions: 44x40.6mm

Capacity: 247cc

Output: 55bhp at 15,000rpm

Carburation: 4x24mm Dell'Orto

Ignition: Mercury magneto

Gearbox: 7-speed with gear primary

Clutch: Multiplate dry

Chassis: Tubular steel duplex cradle

Suspension:
Front: 35mm Ceriani telescopic forks
Rear: Tubular steel swingarm with twin Ceriani units

Brakes:
Front: 210mm four leading-shoe Ceriani drum
Rear: 190mm twin leading-shoe Fontana drum

Weight: 116kg

Top speed: 146mph

Year of construction: 1966

CZ 125

Peter Podesser from Switzerland speeds his 125cc CZ round Monza.

CZ

125

Though outwardly fraternal socialist comrades under the Communist regime of the time, the Czech CZ and Jawa factories were in fact keen rivals in the road racing sphere during the 1960s. Each had their own additional areas of excellence, Jawa in oval racing of all kinds and enduro events, CZ in motocross. From 1956 to 1970, both the factories tilted at the Japanese windmills in a quixotic attempt to find Grand Prix fortune, though invariably their much smaller resources compared to the oriental teams left them condemned to play a supporting role in the no-holds-barred conflict between East and West.

CZ designer Jaroslav Walter's first effort for the 125 class was an Italianate dohc single with gear drive to the camshafts, but in 1962 he produced a new machine with revised camshaft operation by shaft and bevel gear in an unusual layout that would become the trademark of the Czech four-stroke racers from both factories. With the new design a

Chunky cylinder dominates the tiny Czech bike.

three-man team of Malina, Parus and Zipek contested the 125 class at all levels, from GP to national racing, during the next two years. But though they dominated international events behind the Iron Curtain, the bikes were not fast enough to shine against the Japanese multi-cylinder four-strokes and increasingly powerful two-strokes –

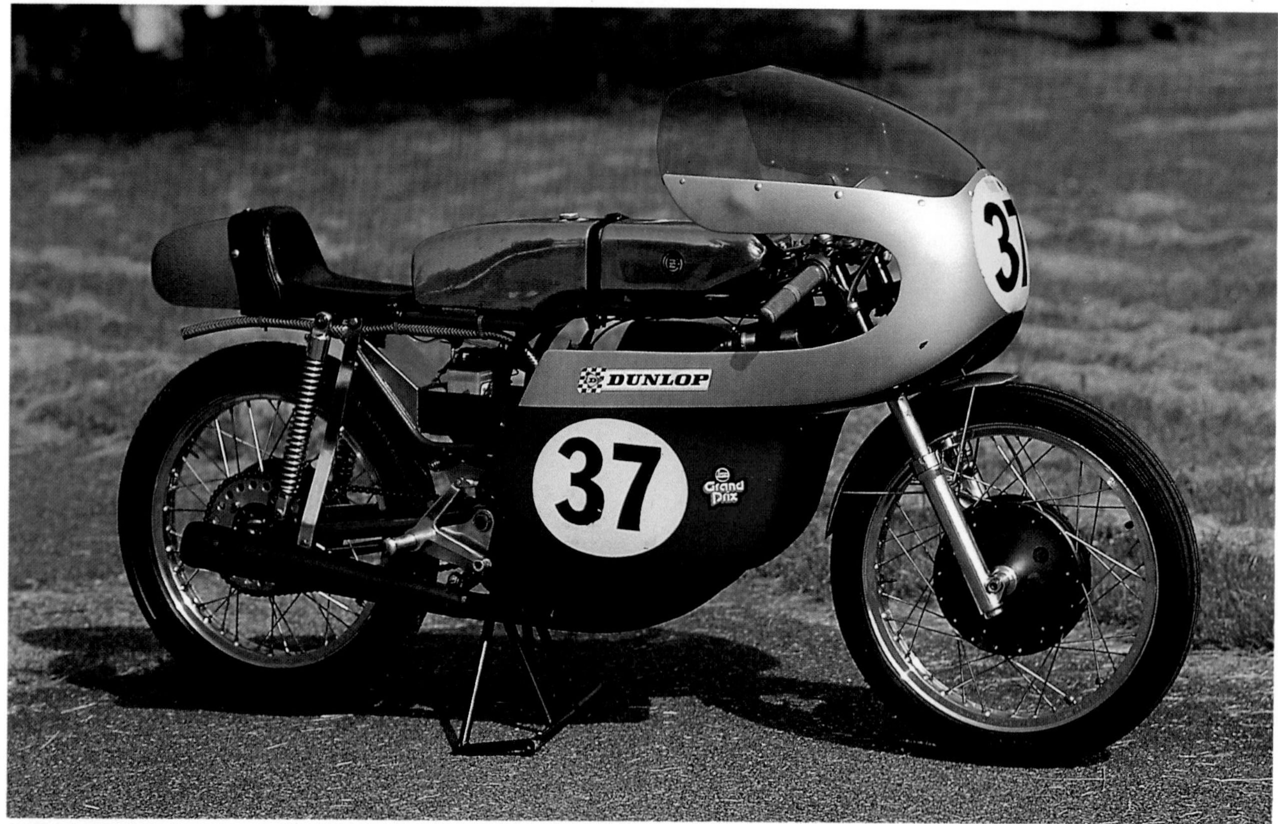

Small but perfectly formed.

CZ 125

nor against the bike the latter were derived from – the rotary-valve MZ from the neighbouring GDR. A pair of sixth places for Malina in the 1962 Isle of Man TT and the 1963 Italian GP at Monza were the best results for the 125cc CZ single, before Walter bowed to the inevitable and produced a twin-cylinder design for 1964. A scaled-up 250cc version and overbored 320cc single – the latter with a distinctive exhaust system with bifurcated pipes – were only a little more successful, though here their light weight against the multi-cylinder designs was more of a factor.

The 125 CZ's air-cooled 55x52mm engine featured trademark Czech valve gear, with bevel drive to the forward, exhaust camshaft directly off the roller-bearing crankshaft with a 2:1 reduction; a second, horizontal bevel shaft ran across the top of the cylinder head to drive the inlet camshaft at the rear. The deeply finned cylinder was inclined forward at 30 degrees to assist the flow of cooling air to its rear, while all engine castings were beautifully executed in electron to save weight. In spite of having

Brakes and forks are CZ's own.

Slim alloy fuel tank permits stretched-out riding position.

Bevel drive from exhaust to inlet camshaft is clearly visible.

just two sodium valves and hairpin valve springs, the little engine revved very high for a single, delivering 20bhp at 12,900rpm – some going for a non-desmodromic two-valve single in the early '60s. Carburation was provided by a 1⅛ inch Amal GP mated to a Dell'Orto float chamber – a concoction fitted to all racing CZs which apparently reduced the tendency for the fuel to froth at high revs. Coil ignition was employed, with twin 10mm plugs, and a six-speed gearbox with gear primary drive, though perhaps surprisingly, in view of the power loss entailed, the multiplate clutch was an oil-bath unit with commensurate problems of drag. With usable power only available from 9500rpm upwards, and in spite of the close-ratio gearbox,

CZ – gunmakers turned motorcycle manufacturers, like BSA . . .

CZ 125

the little CZ had to be ridden like a two-stroke, with much abuse of the clutch to persuade it into the power band out of slow corners. Almost inevitably, clutch trouble was a constant CZ problem, as was the time-consuming task of shimming the no less than eight bevel gears in the camshaft drive.

Unlike Walter's first mid-'50s design, the later 125 CZ single's chassis was not a small-scale twin-loop Featherbed-type frame but an open-cradle type in which the engine was used as a semi-stressed member. The purpose of this was to reduce weight to the minimum, so that the perfectly scaled-down mini-GP racer weighed just 78kg ready to race, aided by a host of beautifully-made lightweight components, such as the two-piece fuel tank, fabricated in narrow-gauge aluminium, or the combined alloy footrest plates, which also double as the swingarm pivot. With a wheelbase of only 1320mm, handling was best described as fingertip-light, but the design of the Czech-made suspension was quite advanced: the 28mm telescopic forks were of the leading axle type and worked effectively, while the rear units had adjustable damping thanks to an external oil feed. The wheelbase could be varied with alternative footrest/pivot plates, too. The little bike was very narrow in order to maximize top speed from the relatively modest power output compared to the rival two-strokes. To reduce external drag the single leading-shoe brakes of CZ's own manufacture copied Guzzi's design in having the operating arms recessed within the backplate, to reduce turbulence around the hubs.

Though like BSA in Britain, FN in Belgium and Sweden's Husqvarna, CZ's main business was making guns (CZ stands for Ceska Zbrovka, roughly translated as Czech Munitions), their little racing four-stroke motorcycles might have come from a watch factory, so beautifully and intricately made were they. Although the CZ 125s were outstanding examples of attention to detail in pursuit of overall weight saving and maximized performance, the whole being achieved on a limited budget, they would have tasted better success in the GP world had Walter been able to produce them five years sooner. Compared to the Japanese multis, the harsh reality was that the CZ 125 was simply not competitive at world level.

Traditional Czech four-stroke engine.

CZ 125

Engine: Dohc air-cooled single-cylinder four-stroke

Dimensions: 55x52mm

Capacity: 124cc

Output: 20bhp at 12,900rpm

Carburation: 1x1⅛ inch Amal GP with Dell'Orto float

Ignition: Dual ignition with 12v battery and twin 6v coils

Gearbox: 6-speed close-ratio with gear primary

Clutch: Multiplate oil-bath

Chassis: Duplex tubular open-cradle

Suspension:
Front: 28mm CZ telescopic forks
Rear: Tubular steel swingarm with twin CZ damper units

Brakes:
Front: 210mm CZ single leading-shoe drum
Rear: 200mm CZ single leading-shoe drum

Weight: 78kg dry

Top speed: 110mph

Year of construction: 1962

HONDA RC166 SIX

Former works Honda rider Ralph Bryans gives a concert aboard the six-cylinder 250 at a Brands Hatch classic meeting.

HONDA

RC166 SIX

Honda's fabulous six-cylinder, which won the 'double double' of four world championships in both 250 and 350cc form in 1966/7 in the hands of the great Mike Hailwood, remains for many enthusiasts of Grand Prix racing the most exotic motorcycle ever built. Though it had two fewer cylinders than the V8 Moto Guzzi a decade earlier, the Honda touched the psyche of lovers of the exotic and unusual the world over, as much for its unmistakable exhaust note, for the miniaturization of its six eggcup-sized cylinders, and for the ease with which it swept to victory in race after race in company with Mike the Bike, as for the sheer fact of being so different and, well, exotic. It's arguable that the performances of this one motorcycle in the handful of years it graced the GP circuits did more for Honda's overall image as a bike manufacturer than all the rest of their racing effort of the era put together. Even today, the sight and sound of a Honda six in action is a guaranteed show-stopper, a three-star feast of GP nostalgia worth a special journey rather than a simple detour.

The six-cylinder Honda's legendary status is all the more remarkable, given that it was conceived in haste, was raced before it was properly track-ready and took more than a year of uphill development before it could be considered truly successful. That Honda stuck at the task of turning the six into a winner is a testament not only to their determination and resources, but also to the character of Mike Hailwood. It was not until he, always a person to speak his mind politely but honestly, told Honda some pretty unpalatable home truths about the way the six-cylinder handled, that they finally

Slim in spite of transverse in-line six-cylinder engine.

did something about it. Established rider Jim Redman was too much a company man, for all his great talent on the track, to have done this. Thus the six's status as a machine that was both exotic *and* successful owes as much to Mike Hailwood's much-underestimated development talents as it does to his brilliant riding.

Honda were the only major manufacturer to wave the four-stroke flag in the smaller GP classes in the 1960s, an insistence born of their commitment to this form of engine on their road bike range. But by the middle of the decade their dominance had been challenged by the increasing reliability of the Yamaha, Suzuki and MZ two-stroke rivals, fuelled in the case of the Japanese by the outflow of tuning secrets from East Germany by the defection in 1961 of MZ's star rider, Ernst Degner. As the climax of the 1964 GP season arrived, Honda's dominance in the 250 class was seriously threatened for

The Honda six raced by Mike Hailwood to win the 1967 world title.

HONDA RC166 SIX

Line of megaphone exhausts is carefully calculated to maximise ground clearance.

the first time by Yamaha, on whose RD56 rotary-valve twin, rider Phil Read was set to win the firm's first world title.

Honda's response was typical both in terms of its nature and the speed with which it was executed. Engine designer Shoichiro Irimajiri began work in June on a six-cylinder replacement to the current Honda 250 four, which through smaller cylinders would be able to attain higher revs and thus deliver more specific power. The first RC166 prototype ran just two months later in August, and was brought to the Italian GP at Monza in September disguised as a four, with one exhaust pipe removed on each side to keep the opposition in the dark until the last possible moment! The amazement when Redman fired up the bike for his first practice lap can be imagined: as a *coup de théâtre* it has few equals in GP history.

Overheating problems prevented Redman finishing higher than third that day, though he did lead initially, and won the Japanese GP the following month to register the six's maiden victory. But though reliability problems with the engine were eventually cured, its handling remained a major problem, which Honda were too overstretched, due to their concurrent involvement in GP car racing for the first time, to rectify. Read won the 250 title again in 1965 for Yamaha, with Redman and Honda a poor second. But for the following season Mike Hailwood replaced Redman as Honda's lead rider in the 250/350 classes, with a much-improved version of the six, now bored as well to 297cc for the 350 class. Hailwood won every 250cc GP in 1966 to make a dramatic and convincing clean sweep of the championship, and also fended off a challenge from Agostini on the new three-cylinder MV to win the 350 crown as well. In 1967, he repeated the double – though Read on the 250 Yamaha V4 pressed him much harder – and with Honda's subsequent retirement

Inclined cylinders are fed by bank of six 17mm Keihin carbs.

Ear protectors, please!

HONDA RC166 SIX

from racing, established the 250/297cc six as perhaps their greatest road racing design.

The in-line 24-valve six-cylinder engine measured 39x34.5mm in 247cc form (41x37.5mm in 297cc guise) and delivered 60bhp at no less than 18,000rpm. The one-piece air-cooled cylinder block was inclined forward 30 degrees for cooling, and carried the gear drive to the twin overhead camshafts in the centre of the engine. Six 17mm Keihin carburettors each with no less than five different jets were fitted, with three sets of ignition points fired by the Kokkusan magneto driven off the camshaft drive. The wet-sump oil system followed traditional Honda practice, with a narrow, deeply-finned sump projecting forward into the airstream, with twin oil cooler in the leading edges of the alloy fairing. The lack of counterweights in the built-up crank gave two-stroke-like power

250cc version of six was outwardly identical to bigger 297cc.

characteristics with minimal flywheel inertia, and a narrow power band made the seven-speed gearbox a necessity. But with a top speed of 153mph in 250cc form and at 355mm across no wider than Read's Yamaha twin, the six-cylinder Honda was an object lesson in pragmatic racing motorcycle design. Irimajiri knew what it needed to restore Honda to a winning position but it took Mike the Bike to put the finishing touches to the machine as well as ride the result as nobody else could. Together, Hailwood and Honda produced a modern masterpiece.

The most desirable racing motorcycle ever built?

HONDA RC166 SIX

Engine: Dohc air-cooled transverse in-line six-cylinder four-stroke

Dimensions: 39x34.5mm

Capacity: 247cc

Output: 60bhp at 18,000rpm

Carburation: Six 17mm Keihin flat-side

Ignition: Kokkusan magneto

Gearbox: 7-speed with gear primary

Clutch: Multiplate dry

Chassis: Open-cradle tubular steel twin-loop frame

Suspension:
Front: 35mm Showa telescopic forks
Rear: Fabricated box-section steel swingarm with twin Showa units

Brakes:
Front: 220mm four leading-shoe Honda drum
Rear: 200mm twin leading-shoe Honda drum

Weight: 120kg

Top speed: 153mph

Year of construction: 1967

AERMACCHI 350

Trademark green livery for the unique Beart Aermacchi.

350

The pushrod Aermacchi single, with its curiously-finned, near-horizontal cylinder, surmounted by knobbly rocker covers sprouting from an oval-shaped crankcase, was one of the most unusual-looking racing motorcycles ever built. But for all its curious appearance, the Aermacchi was a popular and dependable production racer which gave good service to private owners in both 250 and 350cc classes in the late '60s, before the advent of the faster but more fickle Yamaha two-strokes ended the four-stroke era in GP racing.

Product of an aviation factory located beside Lake Varese in northern Italy, whose racing seaplanes were leading contestants in the Schneider Trophy races of the late '20s, the racing Aermacchis were born from the avant-garde, fully-enclosed 175cc Chimera runabout designed by Alfredo Bianchi, which first appeared in 1956. The Chimera's horizontal single-cylinder pushrod engine later found its way into a more sporting machine, the Ala d'Oro roadster, which began contesting 175cc production races in Italy from 1959 onwards, achieving most success in the hands of a future GP star, Alberto Pagani, son of world champion Nello. In 1960 a 250cc version made its GP debut at the German GP in longstroke (66x72mm) form, before

Reknowned Norton tuner Francis Beart switched to the Italian single in the mid-60s.

AERMACCHI 350

appearing for the 1962 season redesigned by Bianchi into a 248cc shortstroke, measuring 72x61mm, but still fitted with a four-speed gearbox (albeit with gear primary drive), oil-bath clutch and a flimsy-looking tubular spine frame from which the engine was suspended. In this form the 250 Aermacchi delivered a claimed 29bhp at 9800rpm, weighed only a little over 100kg but proved rather fragile in both the chassis and engine department: it had outgrown its roadster heritage.

Accordingly, Bianchi completely revamped the design over the next three years without departing from the basic concept of a light, low, easily-maintained and deceptively simply design which in 350cc form would come to displace the elderly British AJS and Norton singles from their role as the favoured mountof the GP privateer. By this time Aer Macchi had sold their motorcycle business to Harley-Davidson, who continued to support racing development, since in 250cc CRS form the Harley Sprint, as the Aermacchi was known in the States, became a race-winning tool in both dirt track and pavement course events in '60s AMA racing.

Fontana brake and Ceriani forks.

Spine frame gave nimble handling.

Distinctive 'double-bubble' fairing was Aermacchi hallmark.

Weight reduced Beart bike.

Bianchi's approach to development was evolutionary, with a five-speed gearbox, dry clutch, outside flywheel, and 74x80mm 350cc version of the pushrod production racer all introduced at various intervals over the next couple of years. The chassis was completely redesigned, too – while still retaining the large-diameter tubular backbone, this was welded to forged uprights incorporating the swingarm pivot and a partial engine cradle which improved the handling immeasurably, thanks to a stiffer engine installation. Most of these developments were tried out first on the works racers ridden by Pagani and Gilberto Milani, which though they never won a GP race in either category, frequently outlasted the faster but more fragile four-cylinder and two-stroke opposition to finish on the leader board of the major classics. In addition, Milani especially was particularly adept at selecting minor international races where he could pocket some useful winnings against other single-cylinder rivals. Meanwhile a series of bitter battles was waged against the works Ducati desmo singles in Italian national racing, in which the Aermacchis usually had the edge in the 250 class, only to find the boot on the other foot in the 350s! But it was in Britain, thanks to the dedicated enthusiasm of importer Syd Lawton, that the Aermacchi flourished most, dominating the 350cc class by the end of the '60s and twice finishing second to Agostini's 350cc MV triple in the 1969 and 1970 Isle of Man Junior TTs, thanks to Brian Steenson and Alan Barnett. That was the closest Aremacchi ever came to winning a world championship race with their four-stroke single, but IoM success came more readily in the amateur Manx GP races, which they won on four occasions, including in 1970 when Chas Brown won the Junior race on the ultra-lightweight Francis Beart-prepared machine, which had previously taken Jack Findley to third place in the 1969 TT.

In 350cc customer form the Aermacchi delivered an honest 37bhp at 8200rpm by the end of the decade, compared with 32bhp at 10,000rpm for the 250: both weighed the same – 109kg dry. But to keep pace with the two-stroke opposition, Bianchi

Horizontal cylinder gave low build and reduced frontal area.

AERMACCHI 350

experimented with various permutations of engine dimensions, especially on the 350 which, in final factory form, had distinctly oversquare measurements of 77x75mm, in which form it delivered 42bhp at 9000rpm. Inevitably, given the bike's light weight and reduced bulk compared to the British singles still packing the 500cc GP grids, which produced very little more power than the 350 Aermacchi, a half-litre class contender was built, first by scaling up the 350 to 382cc (78x80mm), then later to 402cc, a small series of which were made for sale to privateers at the end of the decade.

A thoroughbred racer derived from a humble roadster.

Might look like a cammy motor, but it's 'just' a pushed engine.

In spite of Kel Carruthers' third place in the 1968 350cc world championship on his Drixton-framed Aermacchi, the day of the four-stroke single was over at GP level. To become truly competitive, Aermacchi had to go with the flow, and though they experimented with an abortive twin-cam version of the horizontal single, they only started winning races once they designed their own Yamaha-like twin-cylinder two-stroke which appeared in 1971, and eventually evolved into the water-cooled machines that, under the Harley label, took Walter Villa to four world titles in the mid-'70s. If you can't beat 'em, join 'em!

AERMACCHI 350

Engine: Pushrod ohv air-cooled single-cylinder four-stroke

Dimensions: 74x80mm

Capacity: 344cc

Output: 38bhp at 8400rpm

Carburation: 1x35mm Dell'Orto

Ignition: 6v battery/coil

Gearbox: 5-speed with gear primary

Clutch: Multiplate dry

Chassis: Tubular steel spine with forged engine cradle

Suspension:
Front: 35mm Ceriani telescopic forks
Rear: Tubular steel swingarm with twin Girling units

Brakes:
Front: 210mm four leading-shoe Fontana drum
Rear: 180mm twin leading-shoe Fontana drum

Weight: 105kg

Top speed: 128mph

Year of construction: 1968

PATON

500 BICILIND

The author en route to winning the 1987 Dutch Historic TT on his 500 Paton.

RICA

PATON

500 BICILINDRICA

Few men have ever dedicated their entire lives so totally to the cause of motorcycle racing as Italian hyper-enthusiast Giuseppe Pattoni. A former side-car racer who was chief mechanic for the Mondial team which won both 125 and 250cc world championships in 1957, and especially responsible for 250 champion Cecil Sandford's single-cylinder dohc machine, Pattoni struck off on his own at the end of the 1957 season when Mondial, in common with Gilera and Moto Guzzi, retired from racing. Ever since then, Pattoni has remained involved in Grand Prix motorcycle racing with machines of his own manufacture, an incredible record of herculean struggle against the odds. In the modern era of GP racing, when budgets are measured in millions of dollars or billions of lire, Pattoni and his equally dedicated son Roberto provide a reminder of the modern road racing world's link with its past when a host of small companies and home constructors, epitomized by the uniquely Italian concept of 'la moto artigianale', pitted their shoestring skills against the major manufacturers. Their joint creation, the 500 Paton, continues to line up on GP grids against the mega-yen creations of Honda, Suzuki and Yamaha, proving that the age of the little man in GP racing is not dead – yet. As a tale of over three decades of unbroken endeavour, the history of the

Ultimate expression of the Italian 'moto artigianale': the 500 Paton twin.

Giuseppe Pattoni.

Ultra-short wheelbase of the 500 Paton is evident.

BICILINDRICA PAT

Tubular spaceframe was built by Belletti in Milan.

Paton in GP racing has no equal.

The first Paton appeared in 1958, the fruit of a collaboration between Pattoni and Linto Tonti, a former Mondial technician who later found fame as the inspiration behind Moto Guzzi's V-twin pushrod road bikes. So called by combining the first couple of letters of their two surnames (Pa-Ton), this initial design was, in fact, a 175cc Mondial fitted with a Tonti-designed dohc cylinder head to replace the standard single-cam top end. A similar transformation took place on a 125cc version which followed soon after and which achieved some renown by launching Mike Hailwood on the path to success in the Isle of Man 1958 125 TT, when he rode it into

Countdown to the 1986 French Historic GP. From front to back Dave Roper (Matchless G50); the author on his Paton; and John Surtees (Norton Manx) and Hugh Anderson (Matchless G50). Roper won.

ON 500

Massive 250mm Fontana front brake fills the wheel.

seventh place in his first race on the island. The following season the first twin-cylinder Paton appeared at the Italian GP at Monza, a 250cc machine ridden by Giampiero Zubani based on a design Tonti had drawn up two years beforehand for Mondial, but never built. This had a massive dohc cylinder head with gear drive up the centre of the cylinders which were inclined forward at 25 degrees, the resultant very bulky engine sitting in a messy-looking trellis frame. The bike was not a success, and the partnership dissolved when Tonti was offered a job by Bianchi to design a trio of twin-cylinder GP racers for them.

This left Pattoni on his own and after a couple of years spent building up capital working for a leading Italian car racer, Giorgio Pianta, Pattoni built an all-new 250 twin which was unveiled at the end of 1963. It was ridden the following season by Alberto Pagani in various GPs, netting a remarkable if fortunate third place in the IoM TT. This established the format for all future four-stroke Patons, with heavily-finned, vertical cylinders, gear-driven dohc, unit-construction six-speed gearbox with gear primary drive and wet-sump lubrication in typically Italian fashion by means of a long finned sump under the engine. The 250 in turn gave birth to a 350cc version which first raced at Vallelunga in 1965 in the hands of Gilerberto Parlotti, then found its way to Britain where it was owned briefly by Mike Duff, before being bought by Liverpool car dealer Bill Hannah for his sponsored rider Fred Stevens to race.

This was the start of Pattoni's most fruitful period, for Hannah was so impressed by the performance of the 350 twin that he encouraged Pattoni to build a 500 version, which duly appeared in the spring of '66 in Stevens' hands. Both machines had a very compact build with a mere 1280mm wheelbase, which made the handling very lively over bumpy

BICILINDRICA PAT

surfaces but also gave acceptably fast handling for a twin. In the hands of Stevens, then after his retirement Billy Nelson, the Hannah-Patons were leading contenders for the honour of first privateer home in late-'60s GPs, with a superior turn of speed to the British singles which were their main rivals, and infinitely better engineered and more reliable than the concurrent Linto. Had those privateers who were unfortunate enough to have their fingers burnt by the Linto settled for a Paton instead, it's probable that they would have enjoyed much greater success, but Pattoni was never the most commercially-minded of people and though he built and sold a total of 10 four-stroke twins over a period of time, these were all effectively hand-built machines constructed by him and his colleague, Gianemilio Marchesini.

The high points of the Paton's career were Fred Stevens' remarkable double in the 1967 North West 200 in Ireland, when he won both 350 and 500cc classes on the Hannah-Patons, while the same year Angelo Bergamonti won the Italian 500cc title on Pattoni's own bike. In due course an eight-valve version of the ultimate 73.5x57.5mm 488cc Paton twin, which in two-valve form delivered 58bhp at the rear wheel at 10,400 rpm by 1969, was developed, and this extended the lifetime of the hand-built twin by another few years; Roberto Gallina and later Virginio Ferrari obtained leaderboard results with the machine well into the mid-'70s. But unlike so many of his contemporaries, Pattoni was able to move with the times and in 1975 Ferrari first rode a new V4 two-stroke Paton, a single-crank design with the outer cylinders pointing at 90 degrees to the inner pair. Years later, Honda paid Pattoni the supreme compliment of copying the same highly unusual layout for their first NSR500 V4 two-stroke. Imitation is always the sincerest form of flattery.

Striking Paton green.

PATON
500 BICILINDRICA

Engine: Dohc air-cooled parallel twin-cylinder four-stroke

Dimensions: 73.5x57.5mm

Capacity: 488cc

Output: 58bhp at 10,400rpm

Carburation: 2x35mm Dell'Orto

Ignition: 12v battery/coil

Gearbox: 6-speed with gear primary

Clutch: Multiplate dry

Chassis: Tubular steel duplex cradle

Suspension:
Front: 35mm Ceriani telescopic forks
Rear: Tubular steel swingarm with twin Girling units

Brakes:
Front: 250mm four leading-shoe Fontana drum
Rear: 210mm twin leading-shoe Fontana drum

Weight: 140kg

Top speed: 150mph

Year of construction: 1968

ON 500

HONDA

RC181 500 FO

The ex-Hailwood 500cc Honda four being exercised at Donington, where it is on display today in the circuit museum.

UR

HONDA

RC181 500 FOUR

As the world's largest motorcycle manufacturer, it seems reasonable that Honda should have coveted the Blue Riband of Grand Prix racing, the 500cc world riders' title. But it's a mark of how difficult it is to achieve such a goal that it took them several tries over two decades before they were able to attain it.

Having dominated the smaller capacity GP classes in the early '60s with a succession of ever more intricate and finely-engineered, high-revving, multi-cylinder four-strokes, Honda eventually turned their attention to the 500cc class in 1966.

Essential massive front brake.

Potent and menacing: Honda's biggest GP four-stroke of the 1960s.

HONDA RC181 500

The machine even Mike the Bike couldn't tame.

But in mounting a challenge to the uninterrupted eight-year reign of the Italian MV Agusta team, they did so not with an air-cooled V8 or an up-rated version of their six-cylinder 250cc design - both of which were mooted - but with a dohc, 16-valve, transverse, in-line, air-cooled four-cylinder which represented the conventional wisdom, according to MV, in the 500 class. More to the point, though, the new RC181 500 four was effectively a scaled-up version of the four-cylinder 350 Honda which had carried lead rider Jim Redman to four world titles in succession up to 1966.

Redman initially spearheaded the Honda challenge for 500cc honours, backed up on occasion by his new team-mate, reigning 500cc world champion Mike Hailwood, recently signed away from MV in a move which might have seriously weakened the Italian team were it not for the maturing brilliance of their new superstar, Giacomo Agostini. But Redman gave the new Honda a dream debut in the German GP, first race of the '66 season, repeating his victory in the second round in Holland - but only by a narrow margin from Ago on MV's new weapon, the 420cc triple. In the third race at Spa the following weekend, Redman crashed in torrential rain and suffered an arm injury which ended his racing career, leaving Hailwood - who had sat out the first race at Hockenheim - as Honda's sole challenger to MV. In spite of three victories on the RC181 during the rest of the season (including the TT), Mike was unable to prevent Agostini winning his first (of 15!) world crowns.

While the RC181 Honda's 57x48mm 490cc engine was undoubtedly very powerful (85bhp at 12,000rpm was claimed for the '66 version, rising to 93bhp at 12,650rpm the next year, both measured at the gearbox sprocket) and fast (Hailwood was trapped at 172mph in practice for the 1966 Belgian GP), it was also extremely unwieldy, even by the standards of multi-cylinder machines of the day. Part of the problem was excessive weight: at its debut the RC181 scaled no less than 154kg dry, later reduced to 141kg with much use of magnesium for the 1967 season, but this alone was not the whole story. Japanese chassis designers had never before been required to harness a crankshaft output of more than 100bhp - the first time this figure had ever been exceeded in road racing, though it was not until the arrival of the 750 Suzuki triple half a decade later that 100bhp or more was actually delivered to the road. Not yet the masters of the black art of chassis design that they would later become, the Japanese did not possess the know-how to build a frame that would steer, handle and brake properly - and in race after race, Hailwood's raw, blistered hands and arms shaking from the effort of mastering such an inherently unstable machine proved this fact.

The 500 Honda four employed the same open-cradle duplex steel frame, using the engine as a semi-stressed member, which was by then accepted Honda practice, mated to a substantial square-section swingarm and 36mm Showa telescopic forks, which had provision for altering the trail by means of an eccentric axle mounting. But no amount of experiment could induce the RC181

Muscular build denoted brute force engineering.

FOUR

Overall layout followed established Honda practice of the time.

HONDA RC181 500

to not weave under power, or understeer in turns, or shake the front end in a straight line – all part of life's rich pageant for riders of modern 150bhp-plus projectiles, but then sufficient to stamp a bike as a 'camel', in comparison to the steady-handling, but underpowered, British singles.

By all accounts that steering damper was needed.

Hailwood persevered with the RC181 for a second season in 1967 – initially with an Italian-built frame which Honda, however, forbade him to race in GPs – and, though runner-up again, came very close to winning the title after a series of titanic struggles with Agostini that are still remembered with awe today. Hailwood's main ally was the powerful yet smooth delivery of the dohc engine which, in an era when 60bhp was the tops for the rider of a Manx Norton, produced 50% more horsepower but with an even wider power band. In its final state of development, fitted with four 31mm Keihin carbs, the RC181 would pull from as low down as 5000rpm, with strong horsepower available from 7800 revs upwards. This gave a 4000rpm power band which, allied with the six-speed gearbox, endowed the Honda with a performance scintillating by the standards of the day. It was too much, really; the chassis technology then available to Honda was no match for their supreme talents for engine design and development. Not that things would change much in the next quarter-century: in 1989, Eddie Lawson's title-winning NSR500 Honda suffered exactly the same problems, although admittedly with almost twice the horsepower!

The heavy gusseting required on the chassis to stop the flex is clearly visible.

HONDA RC181 500 FOUR

Engine: Dohc air-cooled transverse in-line four-cylinder four-stroke

Dimensions: 57x48mm

Capacity: 490cc

Output: 93bhp at 12,650rpm

Carburation: 4x30mm Keihin

Ignition: Kokkusan magneto

Gearbox: 6-speed with gear primary

Clutch: Multiplate dry

Chassis: Tubular steel open-cradle duplex

Suspension:
Front: 36mm Showa telescopic forks
Rear: Steel box-section swingarm with twin Showa units

Brakes:
Front: 240mm four leading-shoe Honda drum
Rear: 240mm two leading-shoe Honda drum

Weight: 141kg

Top speed: 172mph

Year of construction: 1967

FOUR

LINTO

500 BICILIND

Handling was not the Linto's strong point - but when it held together it was fast.

RICA

500 BICILINDRICA

The lot of a privateer in the 500cc class has always been a hard one, no less so 20 years ago than it is today. In the late '60s the hard-pressed riders mounted on increasingly elderly Norton and Matchless singles who comprised the bulk of the Continental Circus were light years away from being able to compete on level terms with the factory multis from MV, Honda or Benelli. Counting on the multis to break down often enough and in sufficient numbers for privateers even to get on the rostrum, let alone win a race, was the worst kind of wishful thinking. Very occasionally it did happen – but only very rarely!

It was a situation ripe for the attentions of an enthusiastic entrepreneur, and Italian enthusiast Umberto Premoli was that man. A former bike racer with a flourishing car dealership near the Aermacchi factory in northern Italy, he realized that a market existed for a small number of purpose-built, twin-cylinder 500cc road racers, with unit construction, gear primary drive and other modern features to provide a practical and competitive

Two Aermacchis equals one Linto – sort of.

Brutal appearance is accentuated by bulky fairing.

alternative to the ageing British production racers. When it first saw the light of day at the end of 1967, the Linto appeared to be just such a bike.

Premoli enlisted the services of former Mondial, Paton and Bianchi designer Lino Tonti to create the bike, which featured a tubular steel spaceframe fitted with the standard Italian brake and suspension kit of the day – Ceriani suspension and Ceriani or Fontana brakes. Called the Linto after its designer, the machine was fitted with a 360-degree parallel twin-cylinder pushrod engine, comprising two 250cc Aermacchi cylinders and heads mounted near-horizontally on a specially-designed magnesium crankcase. Essentially, every piece outside the crankcase mouth, including the conrods and pistons, was a production Aermacchi component (in an effort to reduce costs and improve supply of spare parts); the rest, including the built-up crankshaft and six-speed gearbox, was made by a variety of specially-commissioned outside suppliers, then assembled in the Linto 'factory' – a brick garage down the hill from Premoli's car showroom. Effectively, the dozen Linto racers built during the 1967–71 period were little more than commercialized versions of the traditional italian 'moto artigianale', built for sale rather than the exclusive use of the constructor.

Fontana brake and Ceriani forks.

LINTO 500 BICILINI

Tubular spaceframe is light and strong.

Delivering 65bhp at 10,000rpm in the 1969 customer form, the Linto offered 20% more horsepower than a good Manx Norton, for only a 10% increase in weight – but only at the expense of a quantum leap in complexity and required maintenance. Though wind penetration was much better than the more upright British singles, thanks to the horizontal cylinders and correspondingly low build, the Linto's substantially improved top speed – it was timed at 165mph, compared to 140mph for a top Norton – was not matched by reliability, earning the bike a reputation for fast but fragile performance. The experiences of Alberto Pagani, who was to remain the 'works' Linto rider throughout the bike's GP career, epitomized the bike's nature: on the Linto's debut at the 1968 Dutch TT at Assen, he retired with a broken exhaust. A week later at Spa, Pagani held second place to Agostini's MV, until the ignition failed. But in the next race, the East German GP at the Sachsenring, the Linto finished second behind the flying MV – but ahead of the slower British singles. Fleet, but fickle – that was the Linto's nature.

Side-by-side Aermacchi cylinders sit on a common crankcase.

These early performances by the works bike were sufficiently encouraging for a number of replicas to be sold, all of which proved sufficiently troublesome for most customers to spend the next couple of seasons wishing they hadn't bought one. The high revs and extreme valve timing employed to extract competitive twin-cylinder horsepower from a pushrod engine were the main culprits, leading

The compact engine houses an extremely complicated internal design.

LINTO 500 BICILIND

to a spate of dropped valves and broken valve springs in early bikes. This was eventually cured, as was initial unreliability of the points ignition, though it was only by fitting a Dansi electronic CDI on Pagani's last works racer in 1970 that this was banished for good. More troublesome was the intense engine vibration, which unlike the rival Paton twin only intensified as the revs mounted, making life very uncomfortable for the rider and causing bits to break off and even the chassis to crack in half: Jack Findlay once finished a race aboard his Linto literally holding the bike together with his arms after the frame had broken beneath him. This was nothing to the most frightening Linto trick, which was to lock up the transmission and throw the rider off when the inadequately designed primary drive failed. Findlay was lucky to survive a 160mph crash at Monza when this happened, and not surprisingly decided he'd had enough of the Linto after that! He was not alone.

Large diameter clutch mates to six-speed gearbox.

Though the Linto was never a good handling bike – the long wheelbase dictated by the horizontal cylinders made it a slow steerer – it evolved in time into a competitive and fairly reliable tool, as witness Pagani's victory in the '69 Italian GP at Imola, Swiss-Hungarian Gyula Marsovsky's second place in the 500cc world championship that year, and Pagani's fifth place in the points table the next year. But this all happened too late: by the time the Austrian gearbox engineer Michael Schaftleitner had redesigned the primary drive to make it reliable, the Linto's reputation as unreliable and lethal was sealed. If only Premoli had not been rushed by his own enthusiasm and that of his potential customers into marketing the Linto before it had been properly developed, the story might have been very different. As it was, all that most of his customers were granted were very brief but frustrating glimpses of the promised land offered by the occasional good result scattered amongst a host of retirements, all achieved at the cost of untold expense. A brave but expensive failure.

LINTO 500 BICILINDRICA

Engine: Pushrod ohv air-cooled parallel twin-cylinder four-stroke

Dimensions: 72x61mm

Capacity: 496cc

Output: 61bhp at 9800rpm

Carburation: 2x35mm Dell'Orto

Ignition: Dansi electronic CDI

Gearbox: 6-speed with gear primary

Clutch: Multiplate dry

Chassis: Tubular steel spaceframe

Suspension:
Front: 35mm Ceriani telescopic forks
Rear: Tubular steel swingarm with twin Ceriani units

Brakes:
Front: 250mm four leading-shoe Fontana drum
Rear: 200mm twin leading-shoe Ceriani drum

Weight: 142kg

Top speed: 150mph

Year of construction: 1970

DUCATI 750 IMOLA

This 1973 works F750 racer eventually ended its racing days in Spain successfully.

750 IMOLA

Paul Smart's victory in the 1972 Imola 200-mile race, unexpected to all but the Ducati team themselves, was a benchmark in the history of the 90-degree V-twin desmodromic motorcycle that today has so many followers around the world, not least, somewhat ironically, in Japan. Yet Smart's legendary Imola victory, in which he led home his team-mate Bruno Spaggiari to score a 1-2 defeat by the Bolognese factory of several of the other works teams contesting the so-called 'Daytona of Europe', was achieved on a bike which was not so very different from the one soon to be released on the marketplace – the much-prized 750SS which so many owners rode on the streets during the week and raced at weekends. It was a true production racer.

Ducati designer Fabio Taglioni's decision to opt for a wide-angle 90-degree V-twin engine when producing Ducati's first series-production large-capacity roadster seems normal enough now, but was decidedly avant-garde then: only Guzzi, with their 120-degree Bicilindrica, had built anything like it in Italy before. Like the Guzzi, the V-twin Ducati was effectively obtained by combining two cylinders from Ducati's existing single-cylinder range on a

Cooling slots in fairing.

This bike has a different chassis from the other V-twin racers, with a choice of three rear axle locations.

DUCATI 750 IMOLA

Rangy and rugged, the Big Duke is the John Wayne of motorcycles.

common crankcase. The result appeared in 1970 in valve-spring form, the 750S, with the single overhead camshaft per cylinder driven by Taglioni's preferred method of a vertical shaft and bevels up the right side of the engine, as on the singles. But a desmodromic version, with positively-controlled valve gear similar to that employed on the desmo singles, was already under development, still retaining a single ohc format with all four opening and closing lobes on the same camshaft, rather than the triple-camshaft design of the late 1950s' works racers.

First, though, Taglioni opted to try out some of his ideas in a 500cc V-twin GP racer which, ridden by Phil Read, Spaggiari, Parlotti and Giuliano, obtained some worthy places in Italian events during 1971, both in two-valve form for twisty circuits and, surprisingly, in view of Taglioni's mistrust of multi-valve technology, four-valve guise for faster tracks. Producing 65bhp at 12,000rpm in the latter specification (63bhp at 11,500rpm as a two-valver), the 500 Ducati was equipped with a British-designed Seeley chassis after the original factory design revealed substantial shortcomings in its handling. Low-slung and long, with a 1430mm wheelbase, it was to form the basis of the future F750 bike, which first appeared in race form in practice for the 1971 Silverstone meeting, ridden by none other than Mike Hailwood.

At this stage the 750 Ducati – very much a scaled-up version of the 500 GP racer, then making its only foreign appearance north of the Alps – was almost untested, so Hailwood decided not to race it at Silverstone. The bike was returned to the factory and completely revamped, not reappearing until

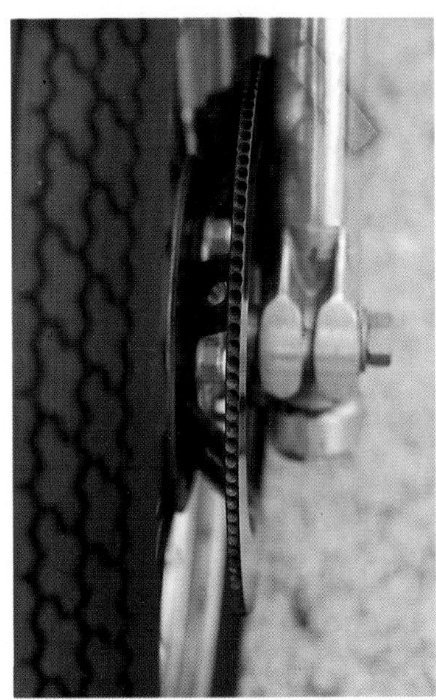

Brake discs are slotted for cooling purposes.

Leading-axle forks were an early-70s fad.

Short-stroke engine produced slightly more power than its predecessor, but only at the expense of tractability.

DUCATI 750 IMOLA

the following spring, when no less than ten works racers were in evidence for the first running of the Imola 200, two each for the four factory riders, plus two spares. Smart's victory amply repaid Ducati's hard development work, as well as proving the benefits of desmodromic valve gear when applied to a large-capacity machine as much as to a smaller single – for the Imola-winning F750 racer was the first V-twin desmo to be produced by the Bologna factory, though its 80x74.4mm 748cc engine was otherwise closely based on the newly-launched V-twin valve-spring roadster. The chassis was similarly close to production, even retaining the lugs for the centre-stand but fitted with unusual Marzocchi leading-axle forks and Lockheed brakes. The build was now decidedly rangy, however, the forward-facing lower cylinder dictating a 1500mm wheelbase, resulting in ultra-stable but rather slow handling which Smart's 'sitting-off' riding style, forerunner of the modern norm, was able to combat.

Though the works 750 V-twin desmos appeared in several minor international events during 1972 with considerable success, the factory team did not reappear *en masse* till the second Imola 200 the following spring. In attempting to repeat their '72 victory, Ducati constructed a series of very special outright F750 racers, which unlike the '72 bike, did not use the 750SS road frame, but an entirely new lightweight tubular chassis whose weight distribution and wheelbase could be varied by means of an eccentric swingarm pivot and three alternative rear axle locations. The engine, too, was completely different, Taglioni deciding to combat the power advantage of the two-strokes which were now beginning to dominate F750 racing by the traditional four-stroke tuning devices of a shorter stroke, more revs, lumpier cams and a higher compression ratio. The new 86x64.5mm engine delivered little power below 6000rpm, but had 4bhp more than the previous design at maximum revs, delivering 89bhp at 10,000rpm, running on an 11.2:1 compression and fitted with twin 40mm Dell'Orto carbs.

In spite of cutting weight by around 10kg to 156kg dry, the short-stroke F750 Ducati racer was no match for the TZ350 Yamaha of Flying Finn Jarno Saarinen in the '73 Imola 200, but proved the equal of the rapidly-developing Suzuki TR750 two-stroke and streets faster than the British Norton twins and BSA/Triumph triples. New Ducati teamster Bruno Kneubuhler looked set to finish second to Saarinen in the first of the two legs which now comprised the race, setting a new outright lap record for the Imola circuit before stepping off at a slow corner and spraining his wrist. This let in team-mate Spaggiari, who finished second overall for the second year running, but the day of the four-stroke in F750 racing was already finished. Ducati's future success with the big V-twin would henceforth lie in endurance and TT F1/Superbike racing, from which the two-strokes were either expressly excluded or handicapped out of contention.

DUCATI 750 IMOLA

Engine: Sohc air-cooled desmodromic 90-degree V-twin four-stroke

Dimensions: 86x64.5mm

Capacity: 749cc

Output: 89bhp at 10,000rpm

Carburation: 2x40mm Dell'Orto

Ignition: 12v battery/coil with two plugs per cylinder

Gearbox: 5-speed with gear primary

Clutch: Multiplate dry

Chassis: Tubular steel open-cradle frame with engine as semi-stressed member

Suspension:
Front: 40mm Marzocchi telescopic forks
Rear: Tubular steel swingarm with twin Ceriani units

Brakes:
Front: 2x280mm Brembo iron discs with Lockheed calipers
Rear: 1x280mm Brembo iron disc with Lockheed caliper

Weight: 156kg

Top speed: 155mph

Year of construction: 1973

SUZUKI TR750

Ex-Sheene/Heron team TR750 in action at Snetterton, having escaped the final appointment with the crusher.

TR750

The early days of Formula 750 saw the Japanese manufacturers produce a number of machines whose inordinate power outputs were more than a match for chassis and tyre technology of the time. The epitome of such fast but unreliable machines was Suzuki's first attempt at an F750 racer, which made its debut in the 1972 Daytona 200, and immediately acquired the unforgettable nickname of the 'Flexi-flyer' as well as a notoriety few other motorcycles have ever equalled.

First road racer to break the 100bhp barrier, first to be timed officially at more than 170mph (Art Baumann *en route* to pole position for that Daytona race with a new lap record of 171.75mph for the full banked tri-oval), the XR 11 Suzuki - better known by its generic model name of TR750 - not only ushered in a new era of two-stroke performance that was all the more remarkable in view of its derivation from the GT750 roadster, but also established its reputation as one of the most evil-handling bikes ever built. The factory's US team of Ron Grant, Jody Nicholas and Baumann had to contend with a machine that was brutally fast by the standards of the day, yet endowed with a chassis so flimsy it could never adequately harness the engine's output. The result was a bike that seduced its riders into a false sense of security with its straight-line potential, before delivering a killer blow to their well-being when the time came to brake and go round corners. To make matters worse, the three-cylinder water-cooled bike was far too fast for the tyres then available. After being politely asked by Dunlop to race their bikes on Goodyears after pre-race testing showed their tyres to be inadequate for the XR 11's speed, Suzuki lost certain victory in the 1972 Daytona 200 when the rear tyre on Jody Nicholas' bike wore through to the cord while he was holding a huge lead, and suddenly deflated - fortunately not on the banking!

Yet within just a couple of years from that inauspicious debut, the XR 11 Suzuki had been developed by the factory's British and Italian dealer teams into a more refined machine whose handling was improved without sacrificing performance. In this

The 'Flexi-Flyer' in its final (and most successful) guise.

Highboy frame had excessive ride height and too much rearwards weight bias.

This engine was closely derived from the GT750 roadster.

guise, it permitted rising star Barry Sheene to win the 1973 FIM F750 world title as well as the British MCN Superbike crown, both run primarily on short circuits where handling was at a premium. Sheene went on to make it a hat-trick of British championships on TR750 Suzukis in 1974 and 1976, finished second in the FIM F750 series in 1975, and in many minds is more closely identified with the Suzuki triple than with any other of the many bikes he rode during his long and illustrious career – in spite of the tyre problems that caused his horrendous Daytona crash on one in 1975. Though by now F750 grids had become all but a sort of Formula Yamaha, the Suzuki XR 11 stayed competitive well into its final season of 1976, when Heron Suzuki rider John Williams confirmed its attributes with a record-breaking victory in the Isle of Man Classic TT race.

Suzuki built two types of frames for the XR 11, both steel tubular twin-shock designs, with the earlier 'highboy' superseded by a lower chassis to which the British Heron team added strengthening struts from the swingarm pivot to the upper top rail to stop them flexing. At the same time the steering geometry was altered to reduce the head angle and trail, and place more weight on the front wheel: rearward weight bias and excessive ride height proved to be

Updated with magalloy wheels and improved steering geometry, the TR750 became a winning bike in Sheene's hands in the mid-70s.

SUZUKI TR750

Watercooled triple made for a narrow bike.

the main reasons for the wayward early handling. But coming at a time when manufacturers were trying to tame 1980s-horsepower with 1960s-chassis design, the bikes always represented something of a compromise, as demonstrated by the flimsy and unresponsive 35mm Showa forks, the narrow wheels and twin rear units, mounted vertically on early bikes, then in a more laydown position later on to give a softer ride. The Suzuki also straddled the bridge between old-style treaded tyres and the racing slicks used today, which became commonplace during its competitive lifetime. More than any other it was this machine which stimulated tyre manufacturers into intensifying development of slicks to cope with 100bhp-plus outputs.

By the standards of GP two-stroke technology of the '60s or today, the TR750 engine was crude but effective, a humble piston-port design with evenly-spaced 120-degree crankshaft throw, that could, however, be tuned to a remarkable extent. Later versions delivered 111bhp from the 70x64mm 738cc engine, at the rear wheel. Though the roadster-derived engine, always equipped with water-cooling which facilitated development in racing form, proved surprisingly tractable low down, competitive horsepower was only produced from 6000rpm upwards, with a safe rev limit of 8200rpm (though power tailed off after 8000 revs) before the conrods would break! Heron Suzuki would gear Sheene's bike for a limit of 7500rpm to give an overrev facility if needed, but this meant a very small power band for such a big engine, making the introduction of a six-speed gearbox for the 1975 season an overdue improvement.

Suzuki paid the price for respecting the spirit as well as the letter of the F750 rules by developing a roadster-based racer that was ultimately no match for the rule-smashing TZ700 Yamaha and its successors. Only the brilliance of Barry Sheene gave it as many race victories as it achieved – even if the 'Flexi-flyer' has its place in history as the first large-capacity two-stroke road racer of the modern era.

SUZUKI TR750

Engine: Water-cooled transverse in-line three-cylinder piston-port two-stroke

Dimensions: 70x64mm

Capacity: 738cc

Output: 111bhp at 8000rpm

Carburation: 3x34mm Mikuni

Ignition: Krober electronic CDI

Gearbox: 5-speed non-extractable with gear primary

Clutch: Multiplate dry

Chassis: Tubular steel duplex cradle

Suspension:
Front: 35mm Showa telescopic forks
Rear: Tubular steel swingarm with twin Ceriani units

Brakes:
Front: 2x270mm Suzuki steel discs with two-piston Suzuki calipers
Rear: 1x250mm Suzuki steel disc with two-piston Suzuki caliper

Weight: 154kg

Top speed: 178mph

Year of construction: 1973

KAWASAKI KR750

Gary Nixon was the moral victor of the '76 FIM F750 title on this Kanemoto-tuned KR750.

KR750

Kawasaki won a world title in the 125cc class with Dave Simmonds on a works rotary-valve twin in 1969, but though in the early part of the next decade they built a series of three-cylinder GP production racers, the two-stroke 500cc HIR, for the next few years the factory's racing involvement was directed at F750 racing with the H2R air-cooled triple, based on the company's fearsomely fast H2 roadster. A combination of the early F750 racer's uncertain handling and its lime green livery which would become a Kawasaki trademark, earned the bike the title of the 'Green Meanie', a machine that few men could tame as successfully as the colourful French-Canadian, Yvon DuHamel, also known as 'SuperFrog'! Though he suffered several spectacular crashes on the 750 triples, DuHamel also brought Kawasaki their first success in big bike competition as part of the factory-backed Team Hansen operation in the USA, winning the 1971 Talladega 200 on the banked Alabama speedway at record speed, repeating the feat in 1972. That year also saw Paul Smart win the richest-ever bike race held to date, the Ontario 200 in California, on a Seeley-framed H2R whose British chassis partially tamed the Green Meanie's bad manners, while Kawasaki took a controversial 1-2 at Road Atlanta after the works Suzukis were disqualified for technical infringements. But 1973 was the best year for Team Hansen in the USA, with the green bikes winning five out of the nine AMA road races - Gary Nixon scored his first wins for the team at Loudon, Pocono and Laguna Seca, while DuHamel won at Charlotte and led a clean Mean Green sweep of the first three placesin the Ontario 200 at the end of the year.

Compact nature of three-cylinder machine is evident here.

After this Stateside success, Kawasaki switched their attention to Europe, where the F750 series had now attained full FIM backing - though stopping just short of a full world championship at this stage. Kawasaki UK were the chosen vehicle, starting their own race team managed by Stan Shenton, with Mick Grant as rider on a factory-supplied H2R in a low-profile learning season in 1974, which ended on a high note when Barry Ditchburn and future Kawasaki-mounted world champion Kork Ballington won the Thruxton 500-Mile race at the end of the season.

Nixon's machine used a special US-built chassis made to Erv Kanemoto's specification.

Wheelbase is short for such a big and powerful bike.

KAWASAKI KR750

Green Meanie in go mode.

Above and right: perhaps the most instantly recognizable colours in bike racing.

This was to be the swansong of the air-cooled H2R, for in 1975 Ditchburn was signed up to race alongside Grant on the new water-cooled KR750 triple, a result of the FIM's decision to drop the minimum homologation figure for F750 machines from 200 road bikes, from which the racer should be derived, to 25 machines of any type. Though still a 120-degree in-line three-cylinder piston-port two-stroke with four transfer ports per cylinder and 'square' dimensions of 68x68mm, the KR750 differed completely from the H2R and was a lot more powerful, delivering 120bhp at 9500rpm, though with a light-switch type power delivery from around 6000rpm that made getting the best from the bike an acquired art. But it was very fast, a fact proved by Mick Grant when he broke Hailwood's long-standing outright lap record in the Isle of Man to leave it at 109.82mph, and was timed at over 180mph on the run down to Brandish Corner from the Creg. Grant and Ditchburn dominated British racing that year, placing 1-2 ahead of Barry Sheene and Suzuki in the British Superbike series, while DuHamel gave Kawasaki a glimpse of the promised land by winning both legs of the Dutch round of the FIM F750 series to take an easy overall victory.

But it was the following season that Kawasaki came closest to achieving their dream of the F750 crown, thanks to the efforts of underfinanced privateer Gary Nixon aboard Erv Kanemoto's KR750 triple. With Kanemoto's engine modifications which

KAWASAKI KR750

KR750 was Kawasaki's last twin-shock works bike.

allowed the engine to rev up to 10,000rpm without loss of power, and using a special frame from the halfway point in the season, Nixon built up an early points lead in the series which seemed to assure him of the title until a post-season FIM jury disallowed the results of the second round in Venezuela (which Nixon had apparently won), handing the title instead to Spain's Yamaha-mounted Victor Palomo. This was pretty shoddy treatment for Nixon's shoestring effort on the lone Kawasaki to challenge the fleet of TZ750 Yamahas.

The KR750 was noticeably narrower but rather taller than its Yamaha rival, even though the fat 24-plate dry clutch intruded some way into the airstream: a six-speed gearbox was fitted, rather than the H2R's five-speed cluster. Located in front of the clutch on the right of the crankcase were the water and oil pumps, as well as a row of triple oil injectors, which fed lubricant under pressure direct from the two-pint oil tank in the seat to each of the three big ends, supplemented by a 30:1 mixture in the fuel. The metering system depended on the type of circuit: on a fast track like the Isle of Man, the metered oiling would be run wide open with the three 36mm Mikuni carbs re-jetted to suit. The oil and water pumps, as well as the mechanical rev counter, were all driven directly off the end of the crank which also drove the Kawasaki CDI ignition. The twin-loop tubular steel chassis had a compact wheelbase for such a big bike of 1365mm, while dry weight was a respectable 140kg.

Kawasaki's last gasp in F750 racing came in 1976. Thereafter the factory concentrated with more success on the 250/350 GP classes with the tandem-twin KRs. The big triples had never really achieved the level of success they had promised, apart from that one British season in '75 and in Australia, where Gregg Hansford and Murray Sayle proved invincible on the Neville Doyle-tuned bikes. But Yamaha had the numbers and, when it came down to it, a better bike in the long term.

KAWASAKI KR750

Engine: Water-cooled transverse in-line three-cylinder piston-port two-stroke

Dimensions: 68x68mm

Capacity: 747cc

Output: 120bhp at 9500rpm

Carburation: 3x36mm Mikuni

Ignition: Kawasaki CDI

Gearbox: 6-speed non-extractable

Clutch: Multiplate dry

Chassis: Tubular steel duplex cradle

Suspension:
Front: 38mm Kayaba telescopic forks
Rear: Fabricated box-section steel swingarm with twin Fox units

Brakes:
Front: 2x296mm Kawasaki steel discs with two-piston Kawasaki calipers
Rear: 1x260mm Hunt aluminium disc with two-piston Kawasaki caliper

Weight: 140kg

Top speed: 180mph

Year of construction: 1976

YAMAHA TZ750

Richard Schlachter in the '82 Imola 200 on Bob MacLean's TZ750.

TZ750

Road racing in the 1970s belonged more than any other machine to the TZ Yamaha in all its various guises, ranging in capacity from 250 up to 750cc: the TA125 twin was a close relation. Without the family of Yamaha's water-cooled production racers, grids would have been thin indeed, not only at GP level but in national and club racing all over the world. Born of the TD/TR air-cooled Yamaha production racer line, first the TZ's 250 and 350cc variants, then later the 700/750 and 500cc designs which sprang from these, packed racing grids from Macao to Monza, Imola to the Island, Daytona to Donington. Over more than a decade, TZ Yamahas at one time or another won just about every major race and took victory at every racing circuit in the world.

The apogee of Yamaha's TZ line was the four-cylinder 750, which dominated not only the short-lived 750cc world championship in the late '70s, but also all forms of large-capacity road racing well into the next decade. But for a bike that was to become so

MacLean's bike as ridden by Schlachter was converted to an American monoshock rear end.

The archetype, much-modified, TZ750.

popular and competitive for so long, the big TZ's debut could hardly have been more controversial; there was even talk at one time of having it banned. For when in 1973 Yamaha engineers Naito and Matsui produced a 700cc version of the factory's works four-cylinder 500cc GP machine, as raced by Jarno Saarinen with so much success before his tragic death, the class they were aiming at was Formula 750, whose rules simply stated that a minimum of 200 machines had to be built and offered to

YAMAHA TZ750

the public. Hitherto this had been a class reserved for racers derived from road bikes, like the BSA/Triumph triples and Suzuki's TR750. But the new Yamaha changed all that, and though its rivals protested that F750 was supposed to be restricted to roadster-based racers, the rules didn't actually *say* that. Yamaha built a very few four-cylinder TZ street bikes with lights, but always intended the model to be a pure racer. They got away with it – and in the process of evolving one of the most successful privateer racers of all time, destroyed the F750 concept as a spectacle of inter-marque rivalry.

The four-cylinder Yamaha racer made its racing debut in the 1974 Daytona 200 ridden by Giacomo

American aftermarket parts are liberally scattered over the Schlachter machine.

The most performance for the least money ever offered to the privateer racer.

Agostini, who was also making his first appearance in the Yamaha team after leaving MV and riding a two-stroke for the first time. The factory OW31 prototype won the Florida classic convincingly, thus joining the select number of models to have tasted victory first time out. That first big Yamaha was actually a 694cc machine, properly known as the TZ700, and effectively created by bolting two sets of TZ350 cylinders to the crankcase of the works YZR500 GP bike. However, unlike the early twins, the TZ four featured reed valves from the very start, though in spite of this the power arrived very suddenly at 8000rpm and peaked at 10,000, at which point around 90bhp was on tap - not a lot by late TZ750 130bhp standards but a lot more than privateers had previously been able to buy off the shelf from anyone. Handling was far from ideal, though not as dangerous as the Flexi-flyer Suzuki, but the twin-shock chassis's flimsy tubular steel structure wasn't really capable of absorbing this sort of horsepower in original, unmodified form.

The TZ700 was fast and dependable from the start: the privateers took to it like flies and it repaid their trust. Jack Findlay won the first FIM 750 title in '74 on one and at the end of that year Yamaha just about wiped out any chance Kawasaki or Suzuki might ever have had of catching up by boring the 64x54mm engine out to 66.4mm for a full 748cc, thus creating the TZ750. Yamaha followed the lead of some of their customers who had already experimented with monoshocking the frame by fitting the 'monocross' cantilever rear end to the 1977 customer bikes, a year in which the 750cc class achieved full world status. Yamaha won all three crowns courtesy of works riders Baker and Cecotto in 1977/8 and Patrick Pons on a production bike in '79, before the FIM scrapped the series for the simple reason that nobody but Yamaha was interested in it. The TZ750 had become a victim of its own success.

This didn't, however, mean the end of the model at international level; the TZ750 continued to live on, especially in the USA where it formed the backbone of AMA racing well into the 1980s. New Zealander Graeme Crosby even won the 1982 Daytona 200 on one, to give Agostini another Florida first in his debut race as a motorcycle team manager. But production had ceased by the end of 1979, by which time around 400 bikes had been built. As many of these were being broken up so that their engines could be used for sidecar racing, the number of active TZ750 'dinosaurs' declined steeply until eventually they just faded away. By then, anyway, most of them had been so completely modified away from their original factory specification that there were not only hardly any two alike, they were also effectively the creations of their loving but often impecunious owners.

As such, there are few other motorcycles in recent racing history for which those who owned and raced them have such a soft spot. Powerful but ridable, fast but reliable, the TZ750 almost certainly represents the most performance for the least dollars (or pounds, or francs . . .) that a major motorcycle manufacturer has ever offered for racing use. Quite a milestone.

Fat exhaust pipes gave surprising degree of torque.

YAMAHA TZ750

Flimsy-looking steel chassis worked well on early-generation slick tyres.

YAMAHA TZ750

Engine: Water-cooled transverse in-line four-cylinder reed-valve two-stroke

Dimensions: 66.4x54mm

Capacity: 748cc

Output: 130bhp at 11,200rpm

Carburation: 4x36mm Lectron

Ignition: Hitachi CDI

Gearbox: 6-speed non-extractable with gear primary

Clutch: Multiplate dry

Chassis: Tubular steel duplex cradle

Suspension:
Front: 38mm Yamaha telescopic forks
Rear: Fabricated aluminium cantilever swingarm with Yamaha monocross unit

Brakes:
Front: 2x300mm Brembo steel discs with two-piston Lockheed calipers
Rear: 1x260mm Yamaha steel disc with two-piston Yamaha caliper

Weight: 160kg

Top speed: 175mph

Year of construction: 1979

MV AGUSTA 500 FOUR

The ultimate racer, four-stroke style: the final version of the four-cylinder MV Augusta.

MV AGUSTA

500 FOUR

The record books show that between their Grand Prix debut in 1949 and their retirement from racing at the end of 1976, the Italian MV Agusta team won no less than 275 world championship GP races and 75 world titles, divided on the basis of 38 riders' crowns and 37 for constructors. No other manufacturer can remotely challenge these achievements, made moreover in every solo class except the specialist 50cc tiddlers: MV won seven 125cc riders' titles, four 250cc crowns, nine times in the 350cc category and no less than 17 world championships in the blue riband 500cc class. To call the MV Agusta 'fire engines' the most successful racing motorcycles of all time is no more than the truth. The fact that in obtaining this unparalleled success they also produced a vast array of technically advanced, yet always pragmatically effective machines, whose very appearance embodied the mystical allure of a Latin race bike, only added to their appeal. For more than a quarter-century, the red and silver MVs epitomized the romantic appeal of motorcycle road racing's sporting soul, the passion and fervour with which a red-blooded Italian team took on all comers with their red-painted motorcycles, triumphing by a combination of skill, bravery, brains and brio. In every way they were the two-wheeled counterparts of the Ferrari car team, transcending frontiers and cultures to acquire a devoted following all over the world, yet at the same time the product of the unflinching determination and boundless enthusiasm of just one man. Ferrari had 'Il Commendatore'; MV had Count Domenico Agusta.

The 500 MV was fitted with US-made wheels and brakes.

Like Aer Macchi, Caproni and Piaggio/Vespa, the

Noise regulations ended the MV as a serious force in GP racing.

Agusta family's aircraft manufacturing concern turned to motorcycle production after World War II as a short-term means of getting back on their feet by helping to satisfy the vast demand for basic transportation in war-torn Italy. But for the eldest son of the company's founder, the deep-seated passion for motorcycle sport that his company's early participation in road races in the late '40s evoked, meant racing was more than a means of promoting MV's always minimal road bike sales. Fuelled by the profits from the helicopter division established soon after World War II, which in due course became the biggest in Europe, Count Domenico Agusta was able to go racing in a manner that other men can only dream of, hiring the best brains to build the best motorcycles and the best riders to ride them in all classes and on all circuits. MV Agusta at one time in the mid-'50s employed no less than 16 different riders simultaneously. Nor was this a well-sponsored, commercially-viable operation: these men were paid salaries out of Count Agusta's own pocket. And nor

MV AGUSTA 500 FC

Oversquare engine delivered 102bhp at 14,000rpm.

did they have to lease their rides, as has become commonplace today. This was a huge enterprise, yet the fruit of one man's total commitment. Only the Japanese have ever matched it – and then for entirely different, commercial reasons.

But more than anything else, it was the manner of MV's departure from the scene that has so endeared them to millions of racing fans around the world, for in defending the ethos of another, less commercially-minded era, they were also the last team to wave the four-stroke flag successfully in GP racing. The quixotic rearguard action fought by Giacomo Agostini, Phil Read and Gianfranco Bonera against the relentless advance of the oriental two-strokes in the early '70s aboard the last four-cylinder MV Agustas to be made, stirred the hearts of racing enthusiasts in a way that has never since been matched. Count Domenico Agusta died in 1971, at the height of MV's dominance of the 350 and 500cc classes thanks to Giacomo Agostini, who won a remarkable 13 world titles on the Italian machines. But Domenico's younger brother Corrado, who succeeded him in control of the factory, vowed to continue in racing, even though the threat from Yamaha in both classes and the later Suzuki 500s, was becoming intense.

MV's team manager Arturo Magni – who remained with MV throughout their time in racing and was largely responsible for their remarkable success – and engine designer Ruggero Mazza responded by replacing the three-cylinder machines which had served Agostini so well for over half a decade and following Honda's traditional route to keep four-strokes competitive against ever more powerful two-strokes, increasing the number of cylinders so as to obtain more power at higher revs. Given the current FIM ban on more than four cylinders (even though MV would have preferred a six, and did in fact make one in prototype form), that meant

Low build reduced frontal area; note massive oil cooler.

reverting to the transverse in-line four-cylinder format with central gear drive to the twin overhead camshafts which MV had first adopted back in 1950 – but in infinitely more modern form, with four valves per cylinder, heavily oversquare short-stroke dimensions, reciprocating weight slashed to the minimum and lots of revs.

The 350 was first for the treatment, making its debut in 52x40.4mm form at the end of the 1972 season, permitting Agostini to clinch the world title again in the face of a determined challenge from Saarinen's works Yamaha. Ago retained the title in '73 after Saarinen's tragic death at Monza, but left MV after a stormy disagreement brought about by his belief that the team were favouring his new team-mate Phil Read at his expense. But in '76 he returned to the fold and rode the 350 MV in its final season of racing, now in even shorter-stroke 53x39.5mm format, in which guise it scored the last-ever four-stroke GP victory before the new FIM noise regulations dictated its retirement. Producing a remarkable 75bhp at 14,800rpm, the shriek of the little MV four was at once both its downfall and its splendour.

The 500cc version of the last MV four was hurriedly produced after the start of the 1973 season, when the new four-cylinder Yamaha was seen to be a major threat. In the event, Read won the title quite easily, repeating the feat the following season by defeating Agostini, who by now was riding for Yamaha, as well as rising star Barry Sheene's RG500 Suzuki. The 500 MV four had now broken the 'ton' barrier, delivering 102bhp at 14,000rpm from its 57x49mm engine, yet was scaling just 122kg dry, 4kg more than the 350. Highlight of the season was Read's brilliant win in the Belgian GP at Spa, where he averaged 211.96kph to lead from start to finish in the fastest GP race ever run. It was, in many ways, the MV Agustas' finest hour.

Financial troubles and increased bureaucratic control meant that MV were no longer masters of their own fate, restricted in what they were able to

MV AGUSTA 500 FC

The 500 four and its equally successful 350 sister.

do to counter the growing threat from the East. After a valiant effort by Read to retain the title on an improved version of the 500 four in 1975 it was, ironically enough, Agostini himself, the man who gave MV Agusta so many 500cc title wins, who ended their unparalleled run of world champion-

The MVs known universally as the 'fire engines'....

The most successful marque in the history of GP racing.

ships. The new noise restrictions, curiously deemed necessary by the FIM in contrast to their colleagues in the car world who to this day have not felt obliged to introduce a similar regulation for F1 car GPs often run on the same circuits as the bike races, were the final nail in the coffin of GP racing's last four-stroke team. Yet though the MVs may be dead, the memory of their achievements and what they represented lives on, reminder of the golden age of motorcycle racing.

MV AGUSTA 500 FOUR

Engine: Dohc air-cooled transverse in-line four-cylinder four-stroke

Dimensions: 57x 49mm

Capacity: 498cc

Output: 102bhp at 14,000rpm

Carburation: 4x31mm Dell'Orto

Ignition: Mercury magneto

Gearbox: 6-speed with gear primary

Clutch: Multiplate dry

Chassis: Tubular steel duplex cradle

Suspension:
Front: 35mm Ceriani telescopic forks
Rear: Steel box-section swingarm with twin Marzocchi units

Brakes:
Front: 2x10 inch Hunt aluminium discs with Lockheed two-piston calipers
Rear: 1x220mm Brembo steel disc with Scarab two-piston caliper

Weight: 122kg

Top speed: 175mph

Year of construction: 1973

SUZUKI RG500

For men only – first of the modern breed of 500cc production GP racers.

RG500

Few motorcycles have enjoyed so long or so illustrious a career at the very top level of Grand Prix racing as Suzuki's rotary-valve RG500 square-four – in almost every way the Manx Norton of the late '70s and early '80s. Winner of four 500cc world championships in factory guise – two with Barry Sheene on the British-entered Heron team bikes in 1976/7, and one each for Marco Lucchinelli and Franco Uncini on the Team Gallina machines in 1981/2, the RG500 (sometimes known as the RGB and/or Gamma) in its various production racer forms was the chosen tool of the privateer ranks for more than a decade. Only the advent of the lighter, more powerful, but also much more expensive RS500 Honda triple in the mid-'80s challenged the Suzuki's long reign as the mainstay of GP grids in the modern era.

The XR45 derivative of the RG500 square-four.

Side-facing carburettors are an inevitable handicap of rotary-valve square-four.

Square-tube alloy chassis followed early-80s fashion.

Unveiled in the 1974 season in prototype form, designated XR 14 by the factory and ridden by Barry Sheene, Suzuki's replacement for their outpaced TR500 water-cooled twins was seen to be a scaled-up version of an earlier design by the Japanese company – the fast but fragile mid-'60s 250cc rotary-valve square-four which earned itself the fateful nickname of 'Whispering Death' by its tendency to seize suddenly without any warning, usually at top speed! Fortunately, though the RG500 had its inevitable teething troubles, it soon evolved into a reliable and effective machine with an unrivalled record of GP success in the 1970s. In due course the original square-four design evolved into a stepped-four layout, still with rotary-valve induction, but in spite of the side-mounted Mikuni carbs, which eventually grew to 38mm in choke size, overall width was relatively narrow thanks to careful design of the internal layout. In the early '80s, Suzuki tried to reduce the length of what was inevitably quite a long engine by rotating the gearbox shafts and other internal modifications: the 1983 works XR45 was thus 7mm shorter than the '82 XR40 title-winner, for example. At the same time, constant development took place inside the engine, five-port cylinders being replaced by seven-port ones, then later a nine-port design, while internal friction was constantly being reduced and power stepped up from the XR 14's original 110bhp at 10,000rpm, to the 124bhp at 10,800rpm of Uncini's 1982 title-winning XR 40. This, like most factory RGs, had a short-stroke con-

SUZUKI RG500

figuration of 56x50.2mm, in contrast to the 'square' 54x54mm dimensions of all the other production bikes built over the years. Though Suzuki also used this bore and stroke on occasion for their works machines, in general they opted for the increased power at higher revs that the oversquare engine could deliver, even though the square motor was better at pulling out of corners due to its superior torque.

Inevitably, thanks to its rotary-valve design, the Suzuki's power characteristics were always quite 'sudden', coming on the power strongly at around 8000rpm with a relatively narrow power band up to peak revs of around 11,000, depending on the year and engine specification. Sheene's early bikes were especially peaky, then, by the standards of the day. Suzuki were able to widen the power band so that the RG was easier to ride than its Yamaha rivals, but later as the new-generation V4s began to display a net horsepower and top speed advantage in the mid-'80s, the Suzuki became less tractable again as the factory's engineers narrowed the rev range in search of more bhp. Eventually, they tried to soften the delivery by joining the universal trend towards reed valve induction - still with the stepped-four layout - but the XR70RV raced by Paul Lewis and Kevin Schwantz in 1986 was not a success. Time had passed by the basic RG500 design, and though it still represented a worthwhile ride for the impecunious privateers making up the bulk of the European championship ranks, at GP and especially factory level, Suzuki themselves recognized the need for a new design, which duly appeared at the end of the '86 season - the RGV500 V4.

The RG500's chassis design also evolved greatly over the next decade or so, beginning with a strong but heavy tubular steel duplex frame that gradually became lighter over the years, and ending with a fabricated aluminium twin-loop chassis that was originally made in square-section alloy tubing. In this form it displayed terrifying instability under power until it was strengthened to reduce flex. This made it almost as heavy as the steel frame it replaced, but the answer was at hand - even if the

Trend towards increased frontal weight bias is already evident in this 1983 bike.

Vying for victory: Randy Mamola (Suzuki - 2) and Kenny Roberts (Yamaha - 3) slug it out at the Strubben horseshoe in the 1982 Dutch TT at Assen.

SUZUKI RG500

factory preferred to ignore it – in the form of the composite-structure 'cardboard box' chassis designed by Nigel Leaper and built by the Heron Suzuki team. The square-four engine's architecture was ideal for this type of design, employing CIBA-Geigy honeycomb M-Board which was first faced with alloy sheet, then later with carbon fibre. In this way the Suzuki's vital stiffness to weight ratio was hugely improved, permitting Rob McElnea to gain a series of creditable top ten results in the 1985 season. But development on the square-four engine had all but ceased – the reed valve option was just a stop-gap measure – and though Heron produced a prototype carbon/honeycomb frame for the RGV, the factory declined to adopt it.

A complete roll-call of some of the riders who competed at GP level on the RG500 in its various forms would fill a page: any bike ridden by such as Mamola, Hartog, Middleburg, Williams, Hennen, Mang, Pons, Baker, Ekerold, Crosby, Ferrari, Herron, Read and so many other illustrious names, quite apart from the three men who won world titles on it, must surely go down as one of the great racing motorcycles of all time. Few would dispute that the RG500 Suzuki was just that.

Square-looking square-four.

SUZUKI RG500

Engine: Water-cooled rotary-valve square-four two-stroke

Dimensions: 56x50.2mm

Capacity: 495cc

Output: 125bhp at 10,750rpm

Carburation: 4x38mm Mikuni

Ignition: Nippondenso CDI

Gearbox: 6-speed extractable with gear primary

Clutch: Multiplate dry

Chassis: Aluminium square-section tubular duplex cradle

Suspension:
Front: 40mm Kayaba telescopic forks with hydraulic antidive
Rear: Aluminium swingarm with Kayaba monoshock unit

Brakes:
Front: 2x310mm AP-Lockheed discs with four-piston AP calipers
Rear: 1x210mm AP-Lockheed disc with two-piston AP caliper

Weight: 117kg

Top speed: 175mph

Year of construction: 1985

XR45's massive radiator indicates emphasis on proper cooling.

KAWASAKI KR350

The author astride the Kawasaki KR350 – undisputed champion of the 350 class.

KR350

Few bikes have ever dominated their chosen class of Grand Prix racing as completely as did the tandem-twin Kawasakis in the 250cc and 350cc categories at world championship level from 1978 to 1982. During that half-decade, the lean 'Green Meanies' won no less than eight world titles and a total of 73 GP races, taking South African Kork Ballington and German Toni Mang each to a pair of 250 and 350 crowns. Moreover, with the demise of the 350 class at the end of the 1982 season, the KR350 Kawasaki has an honour shared by few other machines - that of retiring as undefeated world champion in its division.

Such success seemed very distant in 1975, when Kawasaki returned to the GP arena with a works bike for the first time since their maiden world championship victory in 1969, in the 125cc class with Dave Simmonds. That little bike had been a rotary-valve twin, but with an across-the-frame design which was very wide due to the enforced

Distinctive viewpoint provided by Krauser-style fairing.

The Lean Green Meanie.

location of the carbs on the opposite sides of the crankcase to each other, and with the rotary valves mounted on each end of the single crankshaft. This increased frontal area affected top speed so for the new 250 engine designer Nagato Sato took an idea from a previous, unsuccessful experiment by MZ and placed the cylinders one behind the other in a tandem-twin layout, with the gearbox further aft. Two single cranks, geared together and contra-rotating to reduce gyroscopic effect and improve exhaust port sealing, were employed, but with the pistons firing alternately in a 180-degree configuration that represented Sato's attempt to spread the torque delivery more evenly.

Though Canadian Yvon DuHamel took an encouraging fifth in the '75 Dutch GP aboard the new Kawasaki, followed by third place in the non-title race at Ontario in California at season's end for Britain's Mick Grant, the first tandem-twin Kawasaki was not a success. The problem lay with the 180-degree crank throw, resulting in extreme vibration which not only sapped the rider's stamina but also gave both engine and chassis components a hard time. Kawasaki sat out the 1976 season while Sato redesigned the engine to cure this problem by the simple expedient of re-coupling the cranks so that both pistons fired together in 360-degree format. The new design first raced in 250 form at the end-of-season Japanese GP and finished second to a

Benefits of tandem-twin cylinder layout are apparent here.

KAWASAKI KR350

works Yamaha.

Kawasaki realized from this that they were now on the pace, and returned in force for the full GP season in 1977, not only in the 250 class but with a new 350 as well, obtained by overboring the 54x54.5mm engine to 64mm for a capacity of 350cc. Mick Grant gave the new bike its maiden GP victory in the mid-season Dutch GP, following with another later in the season in Sweden, but it was not until the following season when Kork Ballington was recruited to the team that the bikes became regular GP winners, not only in his hands but also in those of team-mates (and rivals) Toni Mang and Australian Gregg Hansford. It was Kork, though, who scored Kawasaki's first brace of 250/350 titles in 1978, repeating the feat again in '79 before passing the baton to Mang. From then until the factory retired from racing at the end of 1982, Kawasaki dominated the two most hotly-contested categories in GP racing: apart from Kork's rugged fellow-Springbok Jon Ekerold and his 350 Bimota-Yamaha in 1980, no other rival had a look in. The supreme 350cc GP racer was a scaled-up version of its smaller relation with identical chassis and very similar powerplant. This had overlapping rotary valves on the left side (accounting for the apparent slant to the one-piece cylinder head and block when viewed from above) to reduce overall length, with the inlet valves fed by a pair of 36mm Mikuni carburettors. The front crankshaft drove the Kokkusan CDI ignition unit mounted on its right end, with the waterpump driven by the same end of

Though not visible here, engine sits slantwise in the frame.

Rotary-valve engine has the pair of carbs mounted side by side on the left.

the rear crank via a skew gear; unusually, coolant was fed to the cylinder head rather than the crankcases as is more common with racing two-strokes, so that it cooled the hot spots around the twin exhaust ports on the five-port cylinders while still at its freshest. Optimum running temperature was 70 degrees, enabling the KR350 motor in its most developed form in the early '80s to deliver a conservative 75bhp at the gearbox, at 11,800rpm.

The beautifully-made chrome-moly tubular steel chassis was designed by Sato's colleague Kinuo Hiramatsu, and followed conventional practice of the time, except that rather than Yamaha's ubiquitous cantilever monoshock rear suspension design, the Kawasaki employed a more modern Uni-Trak rocker-arm system offering a full rising rate. This may have been a key factor in the KR's perceived handling advantage in its heyday, though by the standards of a decade later the flimsy and unsophisticated 36mm forks, which offered no external means of adjustment, were a limiting factor. Also, the Kawasaki eschewed more radical ideas of forward weight distribution and reduced trail in the steering geometry which were then becoming fashionable. In many ways, the frame was a bridge between the unrefined, hard-to-handle designs of the '70s and the more sophisticated aluminium chassis of the '80s. But by paying great attention to weight-saving detail, Kawasaki produced a machine that scaled a

Single front disc helped slash overall weight to only 104kg.

KAWASAKI KR350

competitive 104kg dry in 350cc form: the single front Bogl & Braun brake disc, where others used two, was a clear example of this philosophy.

The KR250/350 Kawasakis won eight world titles against stern opposition for three reasons: one, no other Japanese factory directly challenged their supremacy in their chosen classes with a full works team; two, they were supremely reliable and easy to work on, making them the bikes that hard-bitten race mechanics still go misty-eyed to recall ten years on and more; and three and most important of all, Kawasaki had the services of two of the finest middleweight riders in the history of GP racing, Kork Ballington and Toni Mang. The success obtained by the tandem-twin Kawasakis is a permanent testament to their talents.

Vertical monoshock rear suspension uses Kawasaki's trademark Uni-Trak linkage.

KAWASAKI KR350

Engine: Water-cooled rotary-valve 360-degree tandem-twin cylinder two-stroke

Dimensions: 64x54.5mm

Capacity: 349.9cc

Output: 75bhp at 11,800rpm (at gearbox)

Carburation: 2x36mm Mikuni

Ignition: Kokkusan CDI

Gearbox: 6-speed

Clutch: Multidisc dry

Chassis: Tubular steel duplex cradle

Suspension:
Front: Kawasaki 36mm telescopic forks
Rear: Aluminium box-section swingarm with Uni-Trak rising rate linkage and monoshock Kayaba unit

Brakes:
Front: 1x310mm Bogl & Braun cast iron disc with two-piston Kawasaki caliper
Rear: 1x210mm Kawasaki aluminium disc/two-piston caliper

Weight: 104kg dry

Top speed: 160mph

Year of construction: 1980

50 BULTACO

Small bike, large rider.

BULTACO

50

The history of the smallest capacity class in Grand Prix racing, the 50cc 'tiddlers', falls into two distinct eras. The first, dating from this class's inception in 1962, saw a titanic duel between the four-stroke Hondas and two-stroke Suzukis, the latter suddenly rendered competitive by the acquisition of MZ technology thanks to Ernst Degner's defection from East Germany complete with a bagful of MZ tuning wizard Walter Kaaden's secrets. Thimble-sized cylinders, as many as two or even three in an engine, turning at up to 22,000rpm, 12 or 14 speeds in the gearbox and a usable power band of as little as 300rpm marked the increasingly sophisticated machines turned out by the Japanese giants in this no-holds-barred struggle.

But then the Japanese departed as quickly as they had come, leaving the 'tiddler' class to become a fertile battleground for European makes and technicians, several of whom would later make their mark at world level in other, larger capacity classes – amongst them Jorg Möller, the German tuner

Electric waterpump above cylinder was battery driven.

Bultaco's title-winner began life in Italy as a Piovaticci.

BULTACO 50

Minimalist engineering of the highest order.

behind the amazing performance of the Dutch-built VanVeen Kreidlers, and Holland's tuning twins, Jan Thiel and Martin Mijwaarts. At the same time, the 50cc class from 1969 onwards became a struggle between these two nations (Holland and Germany), the remarkable Spanish Derbis, and a succession of handmade specials from Italy. No bike draws these various strands together so closely as the monocoque Bultaco which took Angel Nieto and Ricardo Tormo to four world titles in various forms between 1976 and 1981.

The disappearance of the Japanese from the GP scene was followed by a change in the FIM regulations for the 50cc class, which was henceforth limited to bikes with just one cylinder and six speeds in the gearbox. Thiel and Mijwaarts were among the first to take advantage of this rule, constructing a series of highly competitive home-built specials called Jamathi which Dutch riders Paul Lodewykx and Aalt Toersen took to a series of GP victories in the 1968–71 period. This success brought the duo to the notice of Italian millionaire Egidio Piovaticci, who brought them to Italy to develop a pair of machines for his rider Eugenio Lazzarini to contest the 50 and 125cc GPs in 1975. Lazzarini finished second in the 50cc world championship that year to tiddler ace Angel Nieto from Spain on the Möller-tuned Kreidler, but at the end of the season Piovaticci's woodworking machinery business ran into financial difficulties and he was forced to sell his motorcycle GP team – including the services of Thiel and Mijwaarts – to the Spanish Motorcycle Federation, Nieto's principal sponsors. The whole operation was transferred to Barcelona and the bikes renamed Bultacos, even though the famous Spanish marque was already in deep financial trouble itself.

This didn't affect this sporting marriage of convenience, and in the next two seasons (1976/7) Nieto took the world crown again on the 50cc Bultaco, with new star Ricardo Tormo adding a third in 1978 to make it a hat-trick of titles for the Thiel/Mijwaarts design. But then Bultaco too went under (but not before building a small series of replicas of the title-winning bike), leaving the Dutchmen out of a job and causing them to move back to Italy to take over Möller's 125cc Minarelli project, later to be baptized Garelli. Tormo ended up with some of the bikes, and in a specially-built chassis took the Bultaco engine to its fourth world title in 1981 before ongoing development by Kreidler and others made the Spanish bikes uncompetitive.

At a time when their rivals, especially Kreidler, were still using tubular spaceframe chassis, Mijwaarts' Piovaticci/Bultaco monocoque design was not only innovative but the first chassis of this type to win a world title in any class. Since the name of the game in the small capacity classes has always been to save weight without sacrificing rigidity, the stainless steel monocoque was especially suited to tiddler racing, with the single-cylinder rotary-valve engine slung beneath the fabricated, ultra-slim frame, which in turn enabled streamlining developed in the Spanish Air Force's wind tunnel to

Stainless steel monocoque was designed by Dutchman Martin Mijwaarts.

Skinny and shrill-sounding but a winner.

BULTACO 50

be fitted tightly around the bare essentials of the bike. The 40x39.5mm single cylinder was almost horizontal, sitting on crankcases milled from a solid billet of aircraft alloy, which, like the piston, were made by Mahle in Germany, whence also came the Hoeckle crankshaft and conrod. Ignition was generally by Spanish-made Motoplat CDI, and the little engine produced 18bhp at 15,500rpm, with usable power from 13,000 revs. The adoption of an extractable gear cluster, rare on larger capacity machines till a decade later, enabled the most to be gained from this output.

Though the earlier Italian-built chassis had ribbed sides for extra stiffness, later monocoques made in Barcelona were devoid of this and enabled Tormo's '78 title-winner to scale 55.5kg dry – just 0.5kg over the FIM's minimum weight limit. With a fabricated steel swingarm whose location could be varied by means of an eccentric pivot, thus enabling the wheelbase and weight distribution of the little bike to be altered easily, the Bultaco 'tiddler' epitomized the attention to detail and innovative design which characterized the engineering in GP racing's smaller classes for so long. In spite of this, those involved in the 500cc class continued to look down their noses at these little bikes: 'not real motorcycles', was the common rejection – but perhaps those who were so casually dismissive of the 50cc machines should have tried riding one at GP-winning speeds! Then they might have begun to appreciate not only the minimalist engineering which lay behind them but also the incredible skill needed to average over 100mph for a 45-minute GP at somewhere like Spa, on a motorcycle weighing less than most human beings, and with a coffee cup-sized cylinder.

Long, thin monocoque permitted stretched out riding position.

BULTACO 50

Engine: Water-cooled rotary-valve single-cylinder two-stroke

Dimensions: 40x39.5mm

Capacity: 49cc

Output: 18bhp at 15,500rpm

Carburation: 1x28mm Mikuni

Ignition: Motoplat CDI/12v battery

Gearbox: 6-speed extractable with gear primary

Clutch: Multiplate dry

Chassis: Stainless steel monocoque

Suspension:
Front: 30mm Marzocchi telescopic forks
Rear: Steel swingarm with twin Betor units

Brakes:
Front: 220mm Zanzani aluminium disc with four-piston Brembo caliper
Rear: 195mm Zanzani aluminium disc with two-piston Brembo caliper

Weight: 55.5kg

Top speed: 115mph

Year of construction: 1977

KOBAS-ROTAX 250

Carlos Cardus, Champion of Europe in 1983, aboard the U-framed Kobas.

KOBAS-
ROTAX 250

The 1980s saw a revolution in Grand Prix motorcycle chassis design, fuelled by a combination of increasing power outputs and rapid tyre development, which rendered the traditional tubular-steel twin-loop frame in all its many variations outmoded. In order to be stiff enough to harness the extra performance from the engines and improved grip from the tyres, the tubular chassis had to be massively braced or made from such wide-diameter material that it also became very heavy. At a time when all teams were also concentrating on saving weight, this was a vital factor, which led many simply to replace their round steel chassis tubes with square-section aluminium ones - invariably with adverse influence on the handling. Increasing the stiffness to weight ratio was the watchword of chassis development for the '80s, and though Yamaha were also working along similar lines at the same time in a partially successful attempt to

Riding position throws substantial part of body weight on bars.

Distinctive livery of sponsor Jacinto Moriana adorns Kobas-Rotax.

KOBAS-ROTAX 250

Kobas employs production tandem-twin Rotax rotary-valve engine in seminal twin-spar alloy frame.

reduce weight without sacrificing overall stiffness on Kenny Roberts' works YZR500, there is no question that the father of the modern GP race chassis, as well as one of the most influential designers of the decade, was youthful Spaniard Antonio Cobas.

After cutting short his studies for an engineering degree in favour of more practical experience working for a local racing car constructor, Barcelona-born Cobas returned to his first love of motorcycles as a freelance chassis designer in the late '70s. His first commercial design was the spaceframe Siroko, a machine with a steel chassis for the 250 class designed to accommodate either Yamaha parallel-twin or Rotax tandem-twin engines, of which a total of 54 were made up until 1981. After leaving Siroko, Cobas freelanced again for a while, producing among other designs the unique Tecfar-Ducati, a one-litre Big Twin with monoshock rear suspension on which Carlos Cardus first made his name by defeating the might of the Japanese multis in the 1982 Spanish F1 championship. Cobas then returned to the 250cc GP class with his mould-breaking Kobas (he was persuaded to call it such by the graphic artist designing the tank logo, who thought it looked better with a 'K'!), whose twin-spar alloy chassis was the prototype for a whole generation of GP bikes from dozens of manufacturers all over the world. Only eight Kobas were built, most with a Rotax engine, starting at the 1982 French GP at Nogaro in the hands of future world champion Sito Pons, who looked set to give the design a fairytale baptism until he crashed out of contention when lying second at half-distance. But Pons made amends in due course by winning the '84 Spanish GP at Jarama on a Kobas-Rotax, the year after his rival Cardus had taken the bike to a hard-fought title win in the increasingly important European 250cc championship.

Raised centre of gravity chassis flouted convention.

Forward weight bias is almost visually evident here.

Their performances on the Kobas eventually led both Pons and Cardus to works Honda rides, while future series of Kobas-Rotax 250s with spaceframe chassis provided the springboard for a whole generation of Spanish riders to enter GP racing with equal success, the most notable being future works Cagiva and Yamaha ace, Juan Garriga. By the end of the decade Cobas' talents had become recognized even by Honda, who permitted him to alter the design of Pons' works NSR250 according to his own ideas – an honour which yielded two world titles for the Spanish star. Meanwhile, though, Cobas achieved due recognition in his own right by gaining his first world title with a machine bearing his name, when teenage prodigy Alex Criville won the 1989 125cc crown aboard the single-cylinder Rotax-powered JJ-Cobas, defeating the might of Honda and Derbi to do so.

The 250 Kobas was an important design not only because it represented the first successful use of the aluminium twin-spar frame design that would become commonplace as the decade wore on, but also because it embodied Cobas' then avant-

Rotax engine configuration lends itself ideally to twin-spar design.

KOBAS-ROTAX 250

garde ideas about chassis and steering geometry, which were also to become conventional wisdom by the end of the '80s. These included positioning the rider so as to throw much of his body weight on to the front wheel in order to improve front-end grip entering a turn, resulting in a 55/45 per cent forward weight bias where other designers of the day were aiming at a supposedly more ideal 50/50 distribution. Cobas also compacted the bike's mass and juxtaposed the centre of mass and centre of gravity to reduce the polar moment and improve handling; he actually raised the centre of gravity to increase weight transference for improved braking and extra traction exiting a turn, and increased rear suspension and rear wheel travel, at the same time controlling these by means of a rising rate linkage carefully calculated to give maximum progression. All these features later became commonplace on GP race bikes, but it was Cobas in the Kobas who first pointed the way. A milestone in modern GP motorcycle design.

Antonio Cobas.

The revolutionary Kobas chassis launched Pons, Cardus and Garriga to GP fame.

KOBAS-ROTAX 250

Engine: Water-cooled rotary-valve tandem-twin two-stroke

Dimensions: 54x54.5mm

Capacity: 249cc

Output: 72bhp at 13,200rpm

Carburation: 2x37.5mm Dell'Orto

Ignition: Motoplat CDI

Gearbox: 6-speed non-extractable with gear primary

Clutch: Multiplate dry

Chassis: Aluminium twin-spar

Suspension:
Front: 35mm Yamaha telescopic forks
Rear: Fabricated aluminium swingarm with White Power monoshock unit

Brakes:
Front: 2x240mm Brembo iron discs with two-piston Brembo calipers
Rear: 1x220mm Brembo steel disc with two-piston Brembo caliper

Weight: 97kg

Top speed: 152mph

Year of construction: 1983

GARELLI

125 BICILIND

At rest in the workshop, Garelli's dominant 125 twin.

RICA

125 BICILINDRICA

Just as the tandem-twin Kawasakis dominated the intermediate 250/350 classes at GP level for more than half a decade, so the parallel-twin Garelli, née Minarelli, ruled the 125cc category – to the point that the FIM was forced to change the class rules to single-cylinder bikes only in a (successful) effort to restore some element of competition. This back-handed compliment to the Garelli's supremacy was prompted by an unbroken chain of seven world titles from 1981 to 1987 in the hands of Fausto Gresini, Luca Cadalora and the great Spanish ace, Angel Nieto, who also won an eighth title on the bike in his first full season aboard it in 1979. The Garelli's engine was designed in 1977 by the so-called 'Wizard of the Two-Stroke', peripatetic German engineer Jorg Möller, who had already penned the 125 Morbidelli machine which dominated the category in the mid-'70s, before being successfully commercialized under the MBA label, in which form it dominated the privateer class ranks

The Moller-designed rotary-valve parallel twin.

Riding a bike this small yet so fast is an acquired art not readily learnt. . . .

for the next decade. But Möller's contract with Giancarlo Morbidelli expired in '77, whereupon his services were snapped up for a reportedly huge retainer fee by the Minarelli company, suppliers of proprietary engines for the hordes of small Italian moped manufacturers, who wanted to improve their low-tech image with some high-tech racing success.

Möller obliged by effectively updating and revamping his parallel-twin, rotary-valve Morbidelli/MBA design, and sending it into battle against his former employers in the green and yellow Minarelli colours. Indication of the effectiveness of his work came with the new bike's victory in its debut GP in Venezuela at the start of the 1978 season in the hands of ex-MBA champion, Pierpaolo Bianchi, but inevitable teething troubles with the new design meant it failed to win the title in its first season.

Instead, it was left to new recruit Angel Nieto to give Minarelli its first world title the following year, repeating the feat in 1981 after Bianchi, now back with MBA again, had recaptured the crown in 1980. This second title, however, was gained with a new monocoque chassis which replaced Möller's original, rather flimsy, tubular spaceframe design.

By this time Möller's contract had expired, so to replace him Minarelli had hired Europe's other two freelance racing two-stroke wizards, Dutchmen

Mechanical antidive linkage fitted to front forks.

GARELLI 125 BICIL

Engineer Jan Thiel talks to rider Eugenio Lazzarini at a Monza test session.

NDRICA

Jan Thiel, the engine man, and chassis designer Martin Mijwaarts, who together guided Nieto to the Italian team's second world title. That completed Minarelli's objectives, so at the end of the season the whole team was sold to the old-established Garelli concern, who repainted the bikes red and black and went on to win six world titles with them under their own name.

Möller's forte was never chassis design, so it was left to Mijwaarts to pen the Garelli's trademark monocoque chassis, first in steel and then later in weight-saving alloy. Initially equipped with twin Bitubo rear suspension units, this was later successfully converted to a monoshock rear end, in which form the whole bike scaled very close to the 75kg class weight limit. Weighing only 6kg but possessing exceptional stiffness in spite of its slim width, the chassis was also robust enough to withstand several successive seasons of title-winning GP competition: only five machines were constructed in total and raced throughout the '80s. Fitted with wind-cheating streamlining developed in the Fiat wind tunnel, the low-slung bike was capable of a remarkable top speed of more than 140mph – but only if the pint-sized rider maximized the benefits of the minimal frontal area by moulding himself to the bike at every opportunity. Nieto's

Angel Nieto winning the 1981 Dutch TT at Assen aboard the Garelli while it was still known as a Minarelli – and painted accordingly.

GARELLI 125 BICIL

Slim monocoque designed by Martin Mijwaarts.

permanently crouched style, honed over many seasons aboard underpowered 50cc tiddlers, made him an ideal companion for the aerodynamic Garelli, a fact reflected in his five world titles aboard the bike in its various guises and names.

Möller's original design produced a compact engine by the standards of a rotary-valve parallel-twin, whose carburettors inevitably add to the overall width of the bike, but Thiel improved on this even more with new crankcases so that overall engine girth minus the pair of 29mm Dell'Orto carbs was reduced to just 355mm. Over a period of time, he also refined the engine still further so that it became both more powerful and more flexible - not an easy combination - even without resorting to the increasingly fashionable use of power-valves. Fitted with a Hoeckle crank, Mahle six transfer/three exhaust port cylinders and pistons, and Krober ignition, the Garelli engine eventually delivered a remarkable 47bhp at 14,600rpm - still the highest specific power output (188bhp/litre) yet attained in GP racing: no wonder it was so successful. But by the standards of small-capacity GP racing, it also displayed considerable flexibility, with strong power available from a little over 10,000rpm, making the fact that the engine had to be dismantled in order to change internal gear ratios less of a handicap.

Mijwaarts' untimely death from cancer in 1988 deprived GP racing of one of its greatest, if least-applauded, chassis designers. Though an exceptional engine developer, Thiel never displayed much talent for building frames, in many ways the root cause of Garelli's later fall from grace once the single-cylinder formula was instituted and they were forced to design a new bike. The Garelli Bicilindrica's total domination of 125cc GP racing for nigh on a decade is a potent memorial to Mijwaarts' talents in the black art of chassis development and also testament to Thiel's abilities to improve on Möller's already refined engine design.

GARELLI 125 BICILINDRICA

Engine: Water-cooled rotary-valve parallel twin-cylinder two-stroke

Dimensions: 44x41mm

Capacity: 124cc

Output: 47bhp at 14,600rpm

Carburation: 2x29mm Dell'Orto

Ignition: Krober electronic

Gearbox: 6-speed non-extractable with gear primary

Clutch: Multiplate dry

Chassis: Aluminium monocoque

Suspension:
Front: 32mm Marzocchi telescopic forks
Rear: Aluminium swingarm with twin Bitubo units

Brakes:
Front: 2x220mm Brembo steel discs with two-piston Brembo calipers
Rear: 1x210mm Zanzani alloy disc with two-piston Brembo caliper

Weight: 79kg

Top speed: 145mph

Year of construction: 1982

NDRICA

EXACTWELD 250

Curvaceous streamlining proved highly effective in maximising top speed.

EXACTWELD

250

A constant feature of Grand Prix motorcycle racing down the years has been the brave but usually fruitless search for success by dedicated enthusiasts to build their own two-wheeled racers and so take on the giants with products of their own ingenuity, time and hard graft. This kind of endeavour was especially common in the immediate postwar era, when money was tight and the supply of over-the-counter production racers limited, even if you had the cash to buy one. But in spite of the growing availability of off-the-shelf machinery, a hard core of dedicated men remained who steadfastly insisted on doing it their way, bikewise, even into the '80s and the era of the repli-racer. No machine epitomized this creative spirit more than the British-built Exactweld, which in winning the 1984 European 250cc championship in the hands of Gary Noel proved that the age of the special-builder was not yet over. At the same time, the Exactweld's success was a testament to the efforts of all the dozens of other home engineers who built their own race bikes over a two-decade period based on the most popular production racer of all time, the TZ250 Yamaha.

Bulbous tank was built in unit with the seat.

Noel's title-winning Exactweld was the most successful in a long line of ever more ingenious and refined specials built by Guy Pearson and John Baldwin, proprietors of the Sussex-based high-precision fabrication business after which the bikes were named. Exactweld's profits from the manufacture of orthopedic tools for the surgical profession, as well as specialist fabrication for the food industry, fuelled a series of 12 finely-crafted racing motorcycles which tasted increasing success at club and national level in Britain from 1978 onwards, culminating in no less than 67 victories in the single 1983 season for Gary Noel on the TZ350-based machine. This encouraged the duo to launch an attack on the hotly-contested European 250cc series the following season, and in true storybook fashion they duly accomplished their target by clinching the title in a nail-biting finale to the season at Assen. It was a victory for the common man and a shoestring style of racing that flourished in the heyday of the so-called Continental Circus in the 1960s, but 25 years later would be all but extinct.

The Exactweld also represented a milestone in GP

Exactweld success gave inspiration to special builders everywhere.

EXACTWELD 250

1
Castrol
EXACTWELD
FERODO
NGK

Stainless steel spine frame gave slim build.

with the Ohlins internals. Similarly, not only were all the fasteners, clutch nuts, crankcase studs and even the carburettor screws in the twin 38mm Lectrons remade in the same material, but the springs in the 38mm Yamaha front forks were also copied in titanium. The cantilever swingarm was fabricated from lightweight Avional aircraft alloy, then almost unknown in Britain for motorcycle use, while further weight was saved by fitting just a single 300mm front disc brake off an RG500 Suzuki, mated to a 10-inch specially-made titanium rear rotor. Cast magnesium Marvic wheels with hollow spokes, only just then becoming available to private teams, reduced weight further, though Exactweld had intended to save even more by fitting their own wire wheels, had they been able to obtain a supply of titanium spokes for them! The whole chassis bristled with technical ingenuity and painstaking, time-consuming labour, culminating in the curvaceous, highly-distinctive streamlining made in a mixture of Kevlar and fibreglass. This

Octagonal spine housed monocross rear suspension unit.

enabled Noel to be clocked at no less than 248kph on the ultra-fast Chimay circuit in Belgium – an amazing speed for a customer K-model TZ250 Yamaha engine without even a factory race kit but only the Exactweld's team's own home-brewed racing design – the first time that a 250cc class machine had to be ballasted to meet the FIM's 90kg minimum weight limit for the category. Even the mega-yen Japanese factory machines had yet to attain this target – publicly, at least. Yet Pearson and Baldwin achieved this goal by ingenuity rather than money spent to buy exotic space-age materials: extensive use of titanium was their only concession to lightweight metallurgy.

The basis of the Exactweld was a hollow, fabricated stainless steel spine frame weighing less than 4kg even with the footrests, and containing the motocross-style Ohlins unit whose alloy body was copied by Exactweld in titanium and refitted

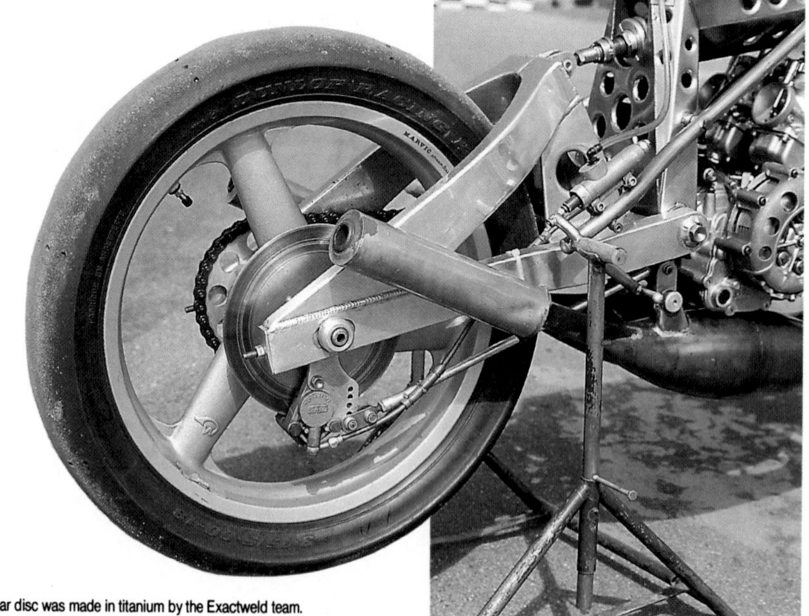
Rear disc was made in titanium by the Exactweld team.

EXACTWELD 250

Standard Yamaha TZ250 engine is underslung from chassis.

engine modifications.

These had concentrated on improving torque and widening the power band, rather than simply increasing engine output, which peaked at just 64bhp at the gearbox, at 12,000rpm. But without the benefit of a powervalve in the early-'80s guise, this TZ engine would pull hard from as low as 8000rpm, yet gave an increasingly vital overrev capability up to 13,000 revs - both areas that would become key aspects of GP engine development by the end of the decade, but which Exactweld were among the first to latch on to, mainly with the aid of Baldwin's own design of laser-cut, TIG-welded exhaust pipes. Coupled with the light 90kg weight (towards the end of the bike's championship season only attained with the aid of some lead strapped to the chassis spine), this endowed the Exactweld with impressive acceleration by any standards of the era.

Strangely, Pearson and Baldwin received almost no recognition for their remarkable feat in Britain, though on the Continent the team was a star attraction of the European and later world championship paddocks. Perhaps because of this lack of interest, their later efforts to develop their own 100 per cent Exactweld racer, a rotary-valve twin with four carburettors which employed the engine as a fully-stressed chassis member, failed to attract the necessary backing to make it viable. These motorcycling prophets remained, sadly, without honour in their own country.

EXACTWELD 250

Engine: Water-cooled piston-port parallel twin-cylinder two-stroke

Dimensions: 56x50.7mm

Capacity: 249cc

Output: 64bhp at 12,000rpm

Carburation: 2x38mm Lectron

Ignition: Hitachi CDI

Gearbox: 6-speed non-extractable with gear primary

Clutch: Multiplate dry

Chassis: Stainless steel spine frame with aluminium engine cradle

Suspension:
Front: 35mm Yamaha telescopic forks
Rear: Fabricated aluminium cantilever swingarm with Ohlins motocross unit

Brakes:
Front: 1x300mm Suzuki steel disc with two-piston Yamaha caliper
Rear: 1x254mm Exactweld titanium disc with two-piston Brembo caliper

Weight: 90kg

Top speed: 155mph

Year of construction: 1984

HONDA NS500

1985 version of three-cylinder Honda 500 employed square-tube alloy chassis.

HONDA

NS500

Japanese companies don't like to lose face by admitting they were wrong, so for Honda to imply this by abandoning the unsuccessful NR500 four-stroke project and building a two-stroke like everyone else, took quite some doing. Well – it wasn't *quite* like the others, for in an age when conventional wisdom dictated the construction of a rotary-valve four-cylinder 500 if you were serious about winning the world title, Honda's perpetual desire to stand out from the crowd led them to build a light, agile, reed-valve three-cylinder: the NS500, their first two-stroke GP racer, if one discounts the MX-derived 125 single clubbie bike.

Honda's abrupt change of policy took place at the end of the 1981 season, after a year in which the NR500 had never looked remotely capable of upsetting the two-stroke applecart. By the start of the '82 season they had a new direction, a new team – reigning world champion Marco Lucchinelli had been poached from Suzuki and paired with shooting star Freddie Spencer, hitherto mostly involved in US Superbike racing – and a new bike.

Honda's compact and lightweight engine.

Works bike had special pipes.

In its very first race in Argentina, Spencer proved how competitive the new Honda was by duelling throughout for the lead with Yamaha riders Roberts and Sheene. Though it took him until the Belgian GP at Spa, midway through the season, before he scored his and the NS500 Honda's first GP victory, Fast Freddie had made his mark. Inevitable teething problems meant the new design wasn't able to win the title in its first season, but in 1983 Spencer made amends by finally earning Honda the maiden 500cc riders' title that the Japanese giant had coveted for so long, after a titanic season-long duel with Yamaha's Kenny Roberts that has gone down in history as one of the closest title chases of all time.

By this time Honda had produced a privateer version of the single-crank, 62.6x54mm, 90-degree V3 machine, with its distinctive format of locating the two outer cylinders pointing upwards and the middle one towards the ground. The RS500 customer bike was only built in very small quantities at considerable cost, but though it differed in many significant details from the NS500 works bikes, it was sufficiently close to them in terms of performance to become the only serious option for a non-works rider trying to get in the points in the 500cc class. A handful were built each winter until 1988, usually incorporating the lessons and modifications embodied in the previous season's works machines.

These were gradually refined and carefully honed over the years, so that even after Honda's introduction of their own V4 in 1984, the NSR500, the triples remained competitive even if they didn't have the same top speed as the fours. Initially the works NS was endowed with a tubular steel frame, but this swiftly gave way to a square-tube alloy chassis which in turn formed the basis of the first RS500s in 1983. In due course, Honda produced a twin-spar aluminium design for the three-cylinder works bikes for 1986, after NS riders Mamola and Katayama had been so disillusioned with the handling of their square-tube chassis that they resorted to sampling non-standard frames from Chevallier and Bakker respectively – an unheard-of move for a works Honda rider, and an opportunity denied Mike Hailwood two decades previously when he sought to remedy the wayward handling of the RC181 Honda 500 four-stroke. The twin-spar frame remedied this problem, enabling

HONDA NS500

Wayne Gardner aviates the front wheel on his NS500 in the '85 Spanish GP at Jarama.

Gardner in more restrained form at the '85 German GP at Hockenheim.

Pierfrancesco Chili to give the Honda triple an excellent farewell to GP racing in works-supported guise, when he took eighth place in the 1987 world championship on the Team Gallina NS500, including a brilliant second place in the rain-lashed French GP at Le Mans in what was the swansong of one of the most significant GP bikes of the 1980s.

The triple's main advantages were its light weight and more nimble handling than the more powerful but heavier four-cylinder machines. However, the engine format dictated that the three 37mm Keihin carbs be located at the front of the engine, pointing directly at the front wheel. With inevitable deflection in spite of the sturdy build of the 43mm Showa forks (whose brake-operated TRAC antidive was the most effective of the various means of combating front-end dive employed by the racing teams around this time, before the introduction of 'upside-down' forks), this prevented the chassis designer from locating the engine as far forward as is ideal and dictated conservative steering geometry if the wheel was not to foul the carbs under braking. Successive riders complained that the NS500 had insufficient weight on the front wheel, leading to understeer and tuck-in problems when braking into a turn, though fitting a 17-inch front wheel instead of the 16-incher initially standardized largely remedied this. Honda eventually built a chassis

Middle cylinder aimed at the ground.

Battery of three 37mm Keihin carbs.

with the engine moved 20mm forward and with a longer swingarm compared to previous models, and in this form Wayne Gardner took the Honda Britain NS500 to fourth place in the 1985 world championship – a result which earned him a V4 factory ride and, two years later, his first world title.

The NS engine was progressively developed over the years, fitted with Honda's mechanically-controlled ATAC power-valve system on all three cylinders (only two on the RS), utilizing flap-type valves in rectangular boxes set into the exhaust pipes. 133bhp at 11,500rpm was claimed for Gardner's 1985 bike, effectively the pinnacle of NS engine development, which was discontinued after this season – about 10bhp more than the RS500 customer bike, but 10 less than the V4 NSR. Though dry weight of the triple was reduced to just 117kg in its final form, this was insufficient to compensate for the power gap against the V4s, making Honda's decision to cover their bets by building their own four (but again just that bit different from everyone else's!) a wise move. But by then, the others had all copied them, for the smooth power delivery of the reed-valve NS engine compared to the more sudden, less controllable nature of the rotary-valve Yamaha, Suzuki and Cagiva opposition, pointed the way ahead for GP engine design. By the second half of the '80s, reed-valve engines were standardized in the 500cc class – a potent testament to the NS500 Honda's innovation.

Twin-spar chassis in 1986 improved handling enormously.

HONDA NS500

Engine: Water-cooled crankcase reed-valve 90-degree V3 two-stroke

Dimensions: 62.6x54mm

Capacity: 499cc

Output: 133bhp at 11500rpm

Carburation: 3x37mm Keihin

Ignition: Kokkusan CDI

Gearbox: 6-speed extractable with gear primary

Clutch: Multiplate dry

Chassis: Aluminium square-section tubular duplex cradle

Suspension:
Front: 43mm Showa telescopic forks with hydraulic antidive
Rear: Aluminium swingarm with Showa monoshock unit

Brakes:
Front: 2x305mm Nissin steel discs with four-piston Nissin calipers
Rear: 1x220mm Nissin steel discs with two-piston caliper

Weight: 117kg

Top speed: 180mph

Year of construction: 1985

KRAUSER 80

Swiss tiddler ace Stefan Dorflinger took two world titles on the Zundapp/Krauser 80.

KRAUSER 80

Spaniard Herri Torrontegui's privateer Krauser won the last-ever 80cc GP at Brno in 1989.

Declining interest in the 50cc 'tiddler' class persuaded the FIM to upsize the category to 80cc for the 1984 world championship to reflect the growing interest in this capacity class worldwide on the road bike front. Quite what this had to do with the rarified world of Grand Prix motorcycle racing was hard to deduce at the time, but the move certainly worked, and for the next six years until the tiddlers were killed off altogether by the vested interests of the big-money teams now dominating the GP paddock, the 80cc class provided some of the most stirring battles in GP racing between the Spanish Derbi team, perennial contestants of small-capacity GP racing, and the German Krausers which, in both works and privateer guise, dominated the class numerically during its brief span of existence. The Krauser in fact began life as a Zundapp back in 1983, the year before the 80s achieved world status, when the European championships' smallest-capacity class was modified to cater for them in an effort to ensure enough new designs would be available and ready for the rigours of GP racing the following season. Only Zundapp took advantage of this, winning the European title with development rider Hubert Abold, which in turn put them in a position to take the inaugural 80cc world championship easily in 1984, courtesy of reigning 50cc title-holder Stefan Dörflinger. But at the end of that year the old-established Zundapp factory collapsed financially, bringing a premature end to the company's successful racing effort. But thanks to German enthusiast and motorcycle luggage manufacturer Mike Krauser, already a noted sponsor of sidecar GP racing, the 80cc project was rescued and reborn under the Krauser name, in which form around 50 bikes were hand-built and delivered to customers over the next half-decade, thus dominating GP and European championship grids throughout the life of the category. Zundapp/Krausers won a total of 13 GP races in total, as well as two world titles – both ridden by Dörflinger – in 1984/5 before the Spanish Derbis asserted their superiority, largely due to the supreme riding talents of their tiddler ace, Jorge Martinez 'Aspar'. Even so, Krauser might well have won the final 80cc world crown, had their young home-grown star, Peter Oettl, not crashed two corners from the end of the final 80cc GP in Czechoslovakia in 1989, to hand the ultimate tiddler title to Derbi's Manual

Mini-cockpit for micro-men.

Single front disc provided ample stopping power.

Herreros. Fittingly, though, Krauser won that last-ever 80cc race, thanks to another Spaniard, Herri Torrontequi, on his privateer Krauser machine.

Zundapp's initial design, later adopted by Krauser, was evolved in conjunction with former 50cc GP rider Herbert Rittberger, whose Rittberger Motor Tuning concern designed and built the prototype bikes, a fact recognized by the 'RiMoTu' logo cast into the engine's single short-stroke 49x42.5mm cylinder. Rittberger subsequently produced all the Krauser works and customer racers on a contractual basis, as well as running Dörflinger's works bikes - a fact which caused some displeasure on the part of customers down the years, since the works engines always had that little bit more performance than the production ones.

Rittberger's design was a classic single-cylinder rotary-valve tiddler engine, with near-horizontal nine-port cylinder and the traditional two-stroke Euro-kit consisting of a Hoeckle crank, Mahle piston and chrome-bore cylinder, and Kröber ignition, powered by a 12v battery which also drove the Bosch electric waterpump. Unlike its Derbi rival, the Krauser's six-speed gear cluster was readily removable for fast ratio swaps - but the choice of alternative gears was in reality rather small, nor was there any option of primary gear ratio. Given that the Krauser engine in its final, developed, form

White Power cantilever suspension unit is located inside the alloy monocoque chassis.

Dorflinger's works Krauser in the pits at Jarama.

Rear alloy Zanzani disc is light but effective.

had a rather small power band by late-'80s GP standards – peak output of the customer bikes was 29bhp at the wheel, at 13,500rpm, but with usable power only from 11,000rpm – this entailed intensive use of the 11-plate dry clutch dominating the right side of the engine. But the engines were easy to work on and, though component life was quite short, they were quite reliable once they had been set up. Carburation with the 36mm flat-slide Keihin carburettor used on later versions was especially unfussy.

The compact engine was initially fitted in a tubular spaceframe, but the customer machines all featured the innovative chassis design adopted by the works bikes from 1985 onwards, in the form of a

Even taller riders can find room for their limbs aboard the spacious Krauser.

KRAUSER 80

riveted aluminium monocoque built by Louis Christen in Switzerland, creator of the bulk of the machines contesting the GP sidecar class for most of the '80s, and winner of countless world titles in the three-wheeler class with chassis built using the same method of construction. The stiff but lightweight and highly distinctive LCR monocoque enabled the Krauser to scale 60kg without fuel as delivered to the customer, fitted with 32mm Forcella Italia forks and a cantilever monoshock rear suspension design, employing a White Power unit. Though 5kg over the FIM's minimum weight limit, this could be further reduced by customers at additional cost but few bothered: instead, they satisfied themselves with the excellent performance and trustworthy reliability that the Krauser gave 80cc habitués. In Britain, it's remembered as the only bike to have permitted a British rider ever to win a British GP in any class, when Ian McConnachie won a thrilling race at Silverstone in '86. But elsewhere, the Krauser is recalled as one of the finest production GP racers of the modern era.

13,500rpm on the Krober revcounter equals 29bhp.

Ultra-compact engine slots neatly beneath the Swiss-built LCR chassis.

KRAUSER 80

Engine: Water-cooled rotary-valve single-cylinder two-stroke

Dimensions: 49x42.5mm

Capacity: 79cc

Output: 29bhp at 13,500rpm

Carburation: 1x36mm Keihin flat-slide

Ignition: Kröber electronic CDI with 12v battery

Gearbox: 6-speed extractable with gear primary

Clutch: Multiplate dry

Chassis: LCR riveted aluminium monocoque

Suspension:
Front: 32mm Forcella Italia telescopic forks
Rear: Fabricated box-section steel cantilever swingarm with White Power monoshock unit

Brakes:
Front: 1x260mm Brembo aluminium disc with two-piston Brembo caliper
Rear: 1x220mm Zanzani aluminium disc with two-piston Brembo caliper

Weight: 60kg

Top speed: 125mph

Year of construction: 1989

CAGIVA V587

1987, and the year that Cagiva came closest to mounting a serious challenge to Japanese 500cc class supremacy.

CAGIVA

V587

The history of motorcycle racing in all countries, at all levels and in all eras is littered with selfless examples of dedicated enthusiasts, who pour untold amounts of time and money into sponsoring their own race team or rider. Without such men, the sport would not exist: it would simply be a business, conducted by major manufacturers for commercial gain and financial profit.

In Italy, though, they go a step further: it's not sufficient just to buy a bike and put your name on the fairing – it has to go on the tank, which means starting your own marque, hiring your own designer, building your own bikes and running your own race team. There's a strong tradition of such personalized sponsorship, which combined with the equally deep-rooted heritage of 'la moto artigianale', has resulted in a number of men, mostly self-made industrialists, returning to their first love of bike racing, taking on the established teams and manufacturers with their own machines – often with surprising success, as witness the countless world titles and GP victories earned by MV Agusta, Morbidelli and FB Mondial, all products of such rich men's passion. So, too, were Piovaticci, RTM, Sanvenero – and Cagiva.

The Cagiva was born in 1978 in the northern Italian town of Varesè, fruit of the enthusiasm of two brothers, Gianfranco and Claudio Castiglioni, who entered Marco Lucchinelli in the 500cc GPs on a modified RG500 Suzuki painted a patriotic red and silver to recall the glory days of the MV Agusta 'fire engines', and renamed Cagiva after their father, **CA**stiglioni **GI**ovanni di **VA**rese. Lucchinelli's success with the bike prompted them to plunge full tilt into the world of motorcycling, purchasing the old Aermacchi factory from Harley-Davidson and re-starting production under the Cagiva name. Within half a decade their energy and commitment had been such that the brothers had effectively built the only serious challenger to the Japanese Big Four on the world stage.

The first proper 500 Cagiva appeared in 1981 in the hands of Virginio Ferrari, an unusual transverse in-line rotary-valve four-cylinder whose tortuous inlet tract and excessive width prevented it from ever being successful. But though the new bike finished only one race that year, it was at least a start, and the mixture of ex-MV race mechanics coupled

Watercooled crankcase reed-valve V4 engine.

with the technical staff from the Aermacchi race shop who had won four world titles just five years previously with Walter Villa on the two-stroke Harley-Davidsons, promised much.

Accordingly, in the first of many subsequent clean sweeps, a completely new machine appeared in 1982, a Suzuki-like rotary-valve square four, which produced 124bhp at 11,500rpm and weighed 137kg, fitted with a square-tube alloy frame to

'La Sfida Italiana' – the Italian Challenger.

CAGIVA V587

Raymond Roche
DISCOVER
BASTOS
CAGIVA
DISCOVER
BASTOS
CAGIVA
MICHELIN

replace the MV-like steel one used in the first bike. With this machine, South African Jon Ekerold gave Cagiva its first world championship point with tenth place at the German GP, and at least by now the Italian-made bike was on a par with the privateer Suzukis. But even with detail improvements, the same machine failed to impress in '83 in the hands of Ferrari, nor with Lucchinelli aboard in 1984, even though horsepower was now up to 135bhp and weight down to 130kg. Internal disharmony within the team saw Frenchman Herve Moineau take over the Cagiva ride in the second half of '84 and he proved that hard riding could still pay dividends by scoring another championship point and recovering team morale. Accordingly, the Castiglionis dug deep into their seemingly bottomless pockets and commissioned yet another new

Twin-spar alloy chassis was multi-adjustable in terms of geometry and set-up.

Marelli ignition offered a choice of advance curves for the first time.

500cc Cagiva engine, this time a reed-valve V4 with twin contra-rotating cranks and initially a 90-degree included cylinder angle, later reduced to 58 degrees for the 1987 season, in which form the bike was known as the V587, ridden by gritty Frenchman Raymond Roche and the matineée idol Belgian, Didier de Radiguès.

The year 1987 was when Cagiva finally seemed to have made the breakthrough, so that instead of

Quartet of carburettors were specially made in Japan by Mikuni.

CAGIVA V587

being consigned to lag behind the Japanese in development terms by six months to a year, they were all but on a par. Both riders scored regular top ten placings with the new bike, which now produced 153bhp at the gearbox, at 11,800rpm, from the 56x50.6mm engine. De Radigués managed a fourth place on merit in the final race of the season, and it seemed that finally the Castiglioni brothers' long-held dream of 500cc GP honours would be realized.

Sadly, it was not to be, for though the following season they signed what appeared to be a race-winning rider in Randy Mamola, four times runner-up in the 500cc world championship, a rash gamble to use Pirelli tyres on the company's return to GP racing after three decades' absence meant that Cagiva could not take advantage of the momentum their promising '87 season had given them.

Gianfranco Castiglioni.

Mamola did make it to the rostrum once, though, finishing third in the rain at Spa to give the brothers their first-ever top three placing, but in general the season was a write-off, and 1989 even worse, again due to lack of direction which saw many changes made to the machine shortly before the start of the GP season. The unflinching determination of the Castiglioni brothers remained undimmed, though, and they vowed to continue the fight. If world titles were awarded on the basis of enthusiasm and commitment, they would already have reaped a hatful.

CAGIVA V587

Engine: Water-cooled crankcase reed-valve 58-degree V4 twin-crankshaft two-stroke

Dimensions: 56x50.6mm

Capacity: 499cc

Output: 153bhp at 11,800rpm

Carburation: 4x35mm Mikuni dual-body

Ignition: Marelli microprocessor electronic CDI

Gearbox: 6-speed extractable

Clutch: Multiplate dry

Chassis: Fabricated aluminium twin-spar

Suspension:
Front: 41.7mm Marzocchi telescopic forks
Rear: Fabricated aluminium swingarm with Ohlins monoshock unit

Brakes:
Front: 2x310mm Brembo discs with four-piston Brembo calipers
Rear: 1x190mm Brembo disc with twin-piston Brembo caliper

Weight: 132kg

Top speed: 185mph

Year of construction: 1987

QUANTEL-COSWORTH

Roger Marshall sweeping to victory in the BoTT race at Spa in 1988.

QUANTEL-COSWORTH

The success of the Battle of the Twins class during the 1980s reflected the enduring need for a road racing category devoid of all but the most basic rules, permitting the dedicated enthusiast to test the merit of his ideas by translating them into metal (or carbon fibre!) and exposing the result to the white heat of competition. The BoTT's two cylinders, four-stroke, anything-else-pretty-much-goes philosophy produced some remarkable and technically advanced four-stroke machines that were Grand Prix racers in all but name. The epitome of these was the British Quantel-Cosworth which won the 1988 Daytona ProTwins race (formerly BoTT, and the unofficial world championship of the class) in the hands of Roger Marshall.

Marshall's victory, as well as his subsequent defeats of the cream of European twin-cylinder racers in later events at Spa and Assen, marked the successful culmination of a five-year effort by an unlikely partnership of a British electronics boffin and an Australian ex-motocross and speedway rider to convert the bike which in many ways embodies the sorry downfall of the British motorcycle industry into a winner – 15 years down the line. The men: Bob Graves, boss of the Quantel digital electronics concern, and Gary Flood, race mechanic par excellence. The bike: the Norton

The ultimate British four-stroke race bike?

Strip-tease.

Challenge, last gasp of the NVT empire, whose engine was designed for them by Keith Duckworth, co-founder of the supremely successful Cosworth racing car engine manufacturers, and accepted worldwide as the leading four-stroke engine designer of his generation. Not by NVT, though, who originally asked him only to design the cylinder head for a new water-cooled dohc parallel-twin 750cc four-stroke that was intended to power the generation of new models that would assure Norton's survival as a manufacturer in its own right in the mid-'70s. The idea was to develop the engine in F750 racing before launching a detuned road version, but as Norton's own engineering staff shrank with the company's decline, so Cosworth were asked to develop more and more of the engine, and eventually the whole thing. Given the piecemeal nature of the commission, as well as a series of inherent compromises in its specification, the result could hardly be called a success. A trio of embarrassingly uncompetitive outings in 1975 were the so-called Norton Challenge's only public appearances before NVT collapsed and the project went down with the company.

But the fact that their abortive motorcycle project was the only Cosworth engine ever developed which had never won a race rankled with Duckworth and his colleagues, and when Bob Graves became a director of the company and expressed an interest in building a bike around the Challenge engine which would rectify that, Cosworth lent him every assistance. The resultant Quantel twin which first ran at Donington in 1985 was at all times a private undertaking by Graves, albeit with Cosworth's advice and Flood's active assistance. The project's target was always to win Daytona, and in 1986 they came very close with flyweight rider Paul Lewis winding up in second

Two giants of British industry, each worldwide leaders in their own field.

Cosworth fuel injection is developed from F1 car technology.

TH

place on the Quantel's American debut. Next year the Quantel returned to the Florida speedway, now ridden by another Australian, Rob Phillis, and fitted with Microdynamics electronic fuel injection rather than the twin 40mm Amal carburettors previously used, in an effort to increase horsepower. But Phillis was unable to come to terms with the four-stroke twin, which suffered from broken balance shafts in practice through being revved too low, and failed to start. But after another season of work, the team returned to Daytona in 1988 with Roger Marshall and an extensively revamped engine, to achieve Bob Graves's dream of ProTwins victory with a bike that was timed at no less than 173mph on the banking.

The born-again Cosworth twin was extensively modified from its original Norton Challenge specification, bored to 90x64.77mm for a capacity of 823cc. Since the 360-degree engine was originally designed for road use, it incorporated a pair of substantial and heavy balance shafts which had to be

Meaty, if massive.

QUANTEL-COSWOR

Roger Marshall.

retained for racing, with belt-drive to the twin overhead camshafts and of course 11:1 Cosworth pistons, four valves per cylinder and a very flat 40-degree included valve angle – all Duckworth trademarks. Surprisingly, the five-speed gearbox (employing a Quaife close-ratio cluster) had a Hi-Vo chain primary drive – a legacy of the piecemeal Norton approach, whereas Duckworth would have preferred gear drive. In Daytona-winning form, fitted with the Microdynamics EFI, the Quantel's Cosworth engine delivered 119.8bhp at 10,000rpm at the gearbox, though later in 1988 one of Cosworth's own fuel injection systems adapted from their car engines with a revised map was installed, which not only gave improved mid-range and a wide power band, but also an extra 5bhp at maximum revs. Even so, to obtain this sort of output from a four-stroke twin, radical valve timing was necessary which meant there was little power below 8000rpm in Daytona form.

Though very heavy, the Cosworth engine was designed to be used as a fully-stressed chassis member, enabling the Exactweld firm, to whom Graves entrusted the task of building a bike around the Cosworth engine, to bolt the front suspension to the cylinder head by means of an alloy fabrication; the swingarm pivoted in the rear of the crankcases, working on a cantilever White Power monoshock unit. This rational design permitted the Quantel to scale 190kg without fuel in Daytona trim – no lightweight, but adequate in light of the impressive power output from the Cosworth engine and sufficient to enable Duckworth's hitherto least successful engine design finally to break its race-winning duck!

QUANTEL-COSWORTH

Engine: Dohc water-cooled parallel twin-cylinder four-stroke

Dimensions: 90x64.77mm

Capacity: 823cc

Output: 125bhp at 10,000rpm

Carburation: Cosworth electronic fuel injection

Ignition: Microdynamics electronic CDI with 12v battery

Gearbox: 5-speed with Hi-Vo chain primary

Clutch: Multiplate oilbath with diaphragm spring

Chassis: Fabricated aluminium front subframe with engine employed as fully-stressed member

Suspension:
Front: 40mm Kayaba telescopic forks with hydraulic antidive
Rear: Aluminium cantilever swingarm pivoting in crankcase with White Power monoshock unit

Brakes:
Front: 2x310mm AP-Lockheed iron discs with four-piston AP calipers
Rear: 1x180mm Brembo aluminium disc with two-piston Brembo caliper

Weight: 190kg

Top speed: 173mph

Year of construction: 1988

DERBI

125 MONOCI

The bike the Japanese couldn't beat, Derbi's 125 mono.

LINDRICA

DERBI

125 MONO-CILINDRICA

The crushing superiority of the Garelli twins in the 125cc class at GP level throughout most of the 1980s, allied with stagnant technical development in the category and the lack of involvement by any of the Japanese manufacturers, persuaded the FIM to scrap the twin-cylinder class rules for the 1988 season, instituting in its place a single-cylinder format that in due course would inevitably kill off the only slightly smaller 80cc category.

But with this one downside, the inaugural single-cylinder 125 world championship in 1988 was a great success, not least because Honda saw a ready market for an uprated version of their MX-derived home-market RS125R club racer, and flooded the grids with the little bikes, as well as running an HRC-backed entry ridden by Italian Ezio Gianola which only just stopped short of being a full works entry. But contrary to pre-season expectations, 1988 was a vintage year for the underdog in the 125 class, with Spain's reigning 80cc world title-holder, Jorge Martinez 'Aspar', winning the inaugural mono-cylinder 125 crown on his rotary-valve Derbi to give the Barcelona manufacturer their ninth world title in two decades.

The only one of Spain's 'big four' to survive the 1980s after Montesa, Ossa and Bultaco progressively slid into bankruptcy and/or foreign ownership, Derbi's undoubted commercial prosperity was built on a solid foundation of racing success. Though they competed internationally from the start of the 50cc 'tiddler'class at world championship level in 1962, it was not till the Japanese pulled out that Derbi began to be successful with their

Tubular spaceframe is light and sturdy.

bright red 'balas rojas' (red bullets), winning their three 50cc world titles courtesy of the great Angel Nieto in 1969, '70 and '72. In 1971 they backed this up with the first of two successive world crowns in the 125 class, obtained as with the 50s by the combination of rider Nieto and in-house two-stroke wizard Francisco 'Paco' Tombas, before dropping out of Grand Prix competition for more than a decade to concentrate on motocross and building up their road bike range.

The controlling Rabasa family judged the time ripe for a return to the GP scene in 1984, with the introduction of the new 80cc formula, with a finely-honed rotary-valve single, housed first in an alloy monocoque chassis, then later in a tubular steel spaceframe. It took two seasons for Derbi to resume their winning ways and defeat the all-conquering Kreidlers, but in 1986 Aspar took the first of

Massive clutch dominates single-cylinder engine.

Rotary-valve single employs 38mm Dell'Orto carb.

DERBI 125 MONOCI

Developed in the Spanish Air Force's wind tunnel.

a hat-trick of 80cc world titles, establishing himself as one of the all-time greats of the tiddler classes. The temptation to move back up to the 125cc class with the introduction of the single-cylinder regulations in '88 was too much for Derbi to resist. True to the record-books they surprised not only Honda but also the rest of the GP establishment, who had tended to regard the small European teams as being a pushover for the first serious effort by one of the Japanese Big Four to wrest their small-capacity supremacy from them.

Tombas and his team based their 125 challenger very heavily on the title-winning 80cc Derbi and to good effect: ample proof of the racing cliché that it's best to scale up a good little 'un. A greater contrast with the reed-valve 'square' 54x54mm Honda with its twin-spar frame and cantilever rear suspension could hardly be imagined, for inevitably Derbi drew heavily on their mountain of accumulated rotary-valve knowledge in designing their first-ever 125 single. Like most great designs, this won its first GP – aptly enough, on home ground at Jarama – and proved to have 'classic' dimensions of 56x50.6mm, with a nine-port semi-horizontal cylinder made by Derbi themselves, though the usual Euro-stroker practice of mating a German-made Hoeckle crankshaft with a single-ring Mahle piston was followed. A side-mounted, flat-slide 38mm

Olé!

Dell'Orto carburettor was employed, feeding the crankcase via a carbon fibre rotary valve – one indication of an area in which Tombas was able to work successfully to extract the 40bhp at the rear wheel, at 12,500rpm, which the little engine delivered. This was the reduction of gyroscopic effect and crankshaft inertia, hence the lightweight rotary valve, for instance, or Derbi's acceptance of the weight penalty entailed in fitting a heavy 12v battery to spark the Motoplat CDI ignition (with the useful extra benefit of saving a fraction of a bhp by powering the waterpump), or the small-diameter dry clutch, smaller in fact than that fitted to their '86 80cc title-winner with three-quarters the power output. But producing Honda-beating horsepower had its drawbacks: in contrast to the accepted

Carbon-fibre canyon. . . .

LINDRICA

World champion Jorge Martinez 'Aspar' on the 125 Derbi – the greatest rider of his generation in the smaller capacity GP classes.

DERBI 125 MONOCI

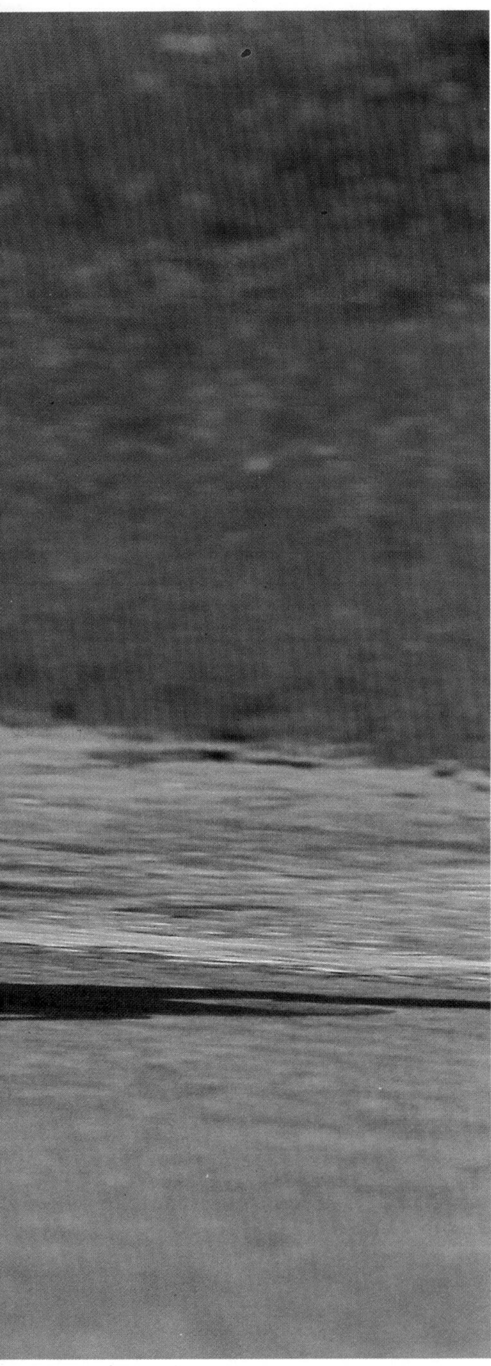

standard among today's GP two-strokes, the 125 Derbi more closely resembled its twin-cylinder forebear that took Nieto to two world titles, by having just a 2500rpm power band, requiring great skill and a special technique from Aspar to get the most out of the little red single's engine.

The spaceframe chassis, with Uni-Trak-type rocker-arm rear suspension using a White Power unit, coupled with the prototype small-diameter inverted forks from the Dutch supplier, enabled him to do this, especially thanks to the massive braking potential on a bike scaling just 67kg – 2kg more than the class minimum – of the twin 250mm Brembo front brakes. Clothed in curvaceous streamlining specially evolved in the Spanish Air Ministry's wind tunnel, the Derbi was the kind of carefully-developed, lovingly-tended product of decades of Grand Prix expertise that even the Japanese found impossible to beat. Few GP observers grudged Derbi their brilliant title win.

DERBI 125 MONOCILINDRICA

Engine: Water-cooled rotary-valve single-cylinder two-stroke

Dimensions: 56x50.6mm

Capacity: 124cc

Output: 40bhp at 12,500rpm

Carburation: 1x38mm Dell'Orto

Ignition: Motoplat CDI with 12v battery

Gearbox: 6-speed non-extractable with gear primary

Clutch: Multiplate dry

Chassis: Tubular steel spaceframe

Suspension:
Front: 36mm White Power inverted telescopic forks
Rear: Steel swingarm with White Power monoshock unit

Brakes:
Front: 2x250mm Brembo alloy discs with two-piston Brembo calipers
Rear: 1x200mm Brembo alloy disc – with two-piston Brembo caliper

Weight: 67kg

Top speed: 140mph

Year of construction: 1989

LINDRICA

APRILIA AF1V250

The closest thing a privateer could buy to a works GP race bike at the end of the 1980s.

AF1V 250

For more than three decades in the postwar era, the 250cc class was the most densely populated at Grand Prix level in terms of the variety of different marques, teams and one-off designs (sometimes using a proprietary engine, on others a motor of their own design) contesting the category. The 250 class represented a battleground where West could still beat East, where a privateer could win a GP or even, as Phil Read did in 1971, for example, defeat a factory team to win the coveted world title. For example, in the 1964 Isle of Man TT, no less than 11 factory teams contested the 250cc race. To take another arbitrary instance, even as late as the 1983 season, there were seven different marques in contention for GP honours, plus a host of Rotax-powered specials. Yet by the end of the decade the most closely-fought class in GP racing had become a straight fight between Yamaha and Honda – and Aprilia, sole survivor of those Eurobikes that were still capable of defeating the infinitely larger Japanese factories for the world championship, as Morbidelli did in 1977.

Aprilia were little more than a moped manufacturer at the start of the '80s, one of the many small Italian companies assembling small-capacity runabouts using a variety of bought-in components. But thanks to the drive of owner Ivano Beggio, who recognized the value of publicity acquired through involvement in racing, by the end of the decade Aprilia had not only become the leading supplier of customer GP machines in Europe, but also vied for the title of Italy's largest road bike manufacturer,

Stands out in a crowded grid, for sure.

APRILIA AF1V250

Arai
KUSHITANI
29
elf

90-degree V-twin engine was designed by Dutchman Dolph van der Woude with the use of Rotax internals. The twin-spar alloy frame is the work of Gaetano Cocco.

with a bright, modern image reflected in the stylish livery and trend-setting styling of its road and race bikes.

Aprilia's position as the largest customer of the Canadian-owned Rotax factory in Austria, themselves Europe's biggest motorcycle engine builder, enabled Beggio to enlist Rotax's help in developing Aprilia's own 250cc V-twin racing engine in the second half of the 1980s. Before that, Aprilia had employed Rotax's proprietary tandem-twin rotary-valve engine for three seasons in a patriotically-painted contender for 250 GP honours, the AF1. Ridden by the perpetually unfortunate Loris Reggiani, this had several times seemed on the verge of making the breakthrough against the might of the Japanese teams, before Reggiani finally won Aprilia's first GP, aptly enough on home ground at Misano in 1987. Aprilia capitalized on this by building a batch of Reggiani Replicas which utterly dominated the hard-fought European championship the following year, occupying the first four places in the final points table in the hands of various Aprilia customers. Meanwhile the factory had already launched its replacement, the 90-degree V-twin, twin-crankshaft AF1V 250. Designed by Aprilia's Dutch race engineer Dolph van der Woude, the AF1V employed Rotax-made internals and cylinders fitted to crankcases and major engine castings designed and machined by Aprilia. This Austro-Italian collaboration produced an engine which was not only more compact than the rather long Rotax tandem-twin unit, but also permitted rear-facing exhausts on both cylinders leading to improved pipe design, allowed use of a larger radiator to reduce engine temperature and consequent power loss, and gave a more compacted mass for reduced polar inertia and improved handling. Though the 54x54.5mm engine, fitted with Rotax's distinctive pneumatic power-valves on the modified cylinders, initially

The 250 was fitted with White Power upside down forks.

APRILIA AF1V250

Ant's eye view of the Aprilia.

yielded only a small 2bhp power increase over the previous Rotax unit, it was not only lighter but also gave chassis designer, Gaetano Cocco, the chance to build a more radical aluminium twin-spar frame, with accentuated forward weight bias as had by then become an important trend in late-'80s chassis design. With the swingarm pivot of the Aprilia V-twin engine 45mm further forward than the Rotax tandem-twin, a weight distribution of 56/44% static could be obtained.

Development of the new bike lagged during 1988 as Reggiani suffered repeated injury, usually in other people's accidents, but by the end of the season van der Woude's team had achieved 78bhp at the rear wheel at 12,200rpm – enough to make the Aprilia the fastest 250 of all in a straight line, even compared to Pons' title-winning Honda NSR. Fourth place for Reggiani in the final European GP of the season in Czechoslovakia seemed to herald a bright future for the Italian V-twin, but though a series of customer versions were built for the 1989 season which once again dominated the European championship, Aprilia surprisingly dispensed with the services of both Reggiani and van der Woude at the end of the '88 season in favour of former Gilera engineer (and another peripatetic Dutchman) Jan Witteveen, and Belgian ex-500 rider Didier de Radiguès. The combination struggled to achieve the same sort of results Aprilia had come to expect, but by contrast German privateer Martin Wimmer shone on his private AF1V 250, earning himself a large degree of factory assistance by mid-season. This underlined the position that the V-twin Aprilia enjoyed as the decade ended – the only machine available for sale across the counter which could enable a private team to compete on an equal basis with the best of the Japanese works 250cc bikes, in an era when GP racing had become almost exclusively the province of the high-tech factory racers – again!

APRILIA AF1V 250

Engine: Water-cooled rotary-valve 90-degree V-twin twin-crankshaft two-stroke

Dimensions: 54x54.5mm

Capacity: 249cc

Output: 78bhp at 12,500rpm

Carburation: 2x38mm Dell'Orto flat-slide

Ignition: Rotax digital electronic CDI

Gearbox: 6-speed extractable

Clutch: Multiplate dry

Chassis: Aluminium twin-spar

Suspension:
Front: 42mm White Power inverted telescopic forks
Rear: Fabricated aluminium swingarm with monoshock Ohlins unit

Brakes:
Front: 2x260mm Brembo steel discs with four-piston Brembo calipers
Rear: 1x190mm Brembo aluminium disc with two-piston Brembo caliper

Weight: 94kg

Top speed: 157mph

Year of construction: 1989

HONDA NSR500

The bike Lawson tamed – enough to win the 1989 World 500cc title.

NSR500

By the end of the 1980s, intensive engine development had pushed the output of the crankcase reed-valve V4 two-strokes that dominated the 500cc class at Grand Prix level to over 160bhp. Harnessing that output presented chassis designers with their sternest test yet, even if this phenomenal increase in horsepower over the years had been matched by a corresponding emphasis on softening the delivery with the aid of computerized exhaust valves and variable ignition curves, and widening the power band. Even so, the NSR500 Honda which Eddie Lawson wrestled to the 500cc world title in 1989 delivered the same horsepower as Hailwood's RC181 four-stroke works Honda 500 two decades previously - but at only 7000rpm: it produced almost twice the RC181's maximum of 85bhp in its 1966 form, at peak revs of 12,000rpm. Grand Prix motorcycle racing design had come a long way in 20 years.

After finally achieving their longed-for goal of capturing the 500cc world title in 1983 with Freddie Spencer and the NS500 triple, Honda changed tack completely the following season, producing the first in the line of NSR500 single-crankshaft V4s, which duly won its debut race at Daytona in Spencer's hands. But a combination of untried components and uncertain handling from the innovative chassis, in which the fuel tank was located under the engine with the bulky exhausts on top, prevented Honda and Spencer from retaining their coveted crown, which went instead, for the first time, to Eddie Lawson on the YZR500 Yamaha.

The most powerful 500cc GP bike ever built - at present!

112-degree single-crank V4 Honda engine has bank of Keihin carbs located between the V of the cylinders.

Honda fought back in 1985 with a more rationally designed conventional chassis which Spencer, in the heyday of his GP career, took to a second title win, thus setting in motion the seesaw exchange of world 500cc championship victories between Honda and Yamaha which would characterize the 1980s. Honda won further titles - in 1987 with Wayne Gardner and 1989 with reigning champion Lawson, who in a shock off-season move had deserted the Yamaha camp he had stayed loyal to for so long in favour of a Honda ride. It paid off - but even he would not have expected to work so hard to retain his crown.

By any standards - but especially those of the neutral-handling, stable Yamaha chassis - the NSR500 Honda demanded more of a rider in terms of skill and bravery than other bikes. The reason was Honda's traditional emphasis on power rather than steering, engine development over chassis -

Nissin front brakes were preferred to AP's carbon stoppers.

HONDA NSR500

a set of priorities which, while it invariably produced the fastest GP performer in a straight line, encompassed certain compromises in its handling. Thus, while the 1989 NSR500's sturdy-looking twin-spar aluminium chassis with its almost obscenely bloated 'hunchback' swingarm appeared strong enough to tame whatever output the V4 engine could deliver, in practice it was insufficiently stiff, and by mid-1989 Lawson's bike had grown an extra layer of metal all around the top of the frame spars, as well as a large-diameter stiffening brace between them, across the top of the engine. Even so, the Honda proved a difficult companion for the reigning world champion, requiring him to race the whole season with the steering damper locked on

Just Like Eddie . . . well, sort of.

The end most other riders saw in '89.

tight to control high-speed instability, in turn making the bike a real handful in slow turns. Also, the NSR500 proved a constant understeerer, necessitating wide, sweeping trajectories in turns where more agile opponents like Schwantz's Suzuki were able to cut corners and turn more sharply. It was a genuine mark of Lawson's talents that he was able to overcome these difficulties and win the title -albeit with only three GP race victories to the more fallible Schwantz/Suzuki combination's six.

Eventually it was Honda's supreme ability to extract more horsepower from their engines than anyone else which really told: in 1989, as in '85 and '87, the NSR500 accelerated quicker and was faster on top speed than its rivals, with a particu-

Aluminium twin-spar chassis was considerably beefed up during the season. 'Hunchback' swingarm gives clear run to exhaust pipes.

HONDA NSR500

larly decisive mid-range advantage in the 8000–12,800rpm rev range, but a smooth transition into the power band from low down. Unlike its twin-crankshaft rivals, the single-crank Honda was a genuine V4, more from a desire to be different than anything else, since the gyroscopic effect of the single crank and extra engine width dictated by it were not ideal. To keep the overall width down, Honda opted for 'square' dimensions of 54x54.5mm (against the 'stack-twin' V4s' 56x50.6mm) and originally disposed the cylinders at 90 degrees, with the bank of four 36mm Keihin carburettors located behind the row of cylinders. In this form, Spencer won the NSR's first title in 1985, but after Yamaha and Lawson regained the 500 crown the following year, the V4 engine was redesigned for 1987 with a wider included cylinder angle of 112 degrees, permitting larger reed-valve boxes and the carbs which fed them to be located now between the cylinders, facing forwards. This not only increased valve area but also gave a more rational line to the exhaust run (further improved with the adoption of the 'hunchback' swingarm in 1988) and in this form Wayne Gardner became the first Australian to win the 500cc world crown in '87. But the following year Honda's almost traditional handling problems reasserted themselves, only barely cured with the introduction of a new chassis for '89, fitted for the first time with Showa's new 'upside-down' inverted forks and, for part of the season at least, the avant-garde AP-Lockheed carbon brakes.

Deeply curved radiator gives optimum engine location.

Honda regained the coveted 500cc world title in 1989 because of the brilliance of Eddie Lawson, aided by their success in taming the substantial power output now extracted from the NSR's V4 engine, and despite the fearsome handling of their umpteenth new chassis produced in the course of the decade. Twenty years previously, even Mike Hailwood had been unable to perform the same miracle with the unwieldy RC181; what would he have made of the bike Eddie rode?

HONDA NSR500

Engine: Water-cooled crankcase reed-valve 112-degree V4 two-stroke

Dimensions: 54x54.5mm

Capacity: 499cc

Output: 162bhp at 12,000rpm

Carburation: 4x36mm Keihin twin-body

Ignition: Shindengen computerized electronic digital CDI

Gearbox: 6-speed extractable

Clutch: Multiplate dry

Chassis: Aluminium twin-spar

Suspension:
Front: 43mm Showa inverted telescopic forks
Rear: Aluminium swingarm with Showa monoshock unit

Brakes:
Front: 2x332mm Nisin steel discs with four-piston Nissin calipers
Rear: 1x196mm Hitco carbon disc with two-piston Nissin caliper

Weight: 124kg

Top speed: 190mph

Year of construction: 1989

INDEX

Illustrations of each machine appear within their separate sections and are indicated by italics.